PRAISE FOR

My Pain-Body Solution

"The tender frankness by which Mike recounts an individual experience of the human truth of pain is truly moving. This story reminds us of two essential features of life: Suffering is an inescapable part of the path, and there is absolutely a way through it."

—**Kali Basman** of Kali Durga Yoga

"*My Pain-Body Solution: A Journey to the Other Side of Suffering* by Michael J. Murray points you toward understanding pain, its personal message, and its ultimate relief. Murray's story is riveting, and it's your story as well. His persistence in tracking down the truth and the inspiring self-awareness that resulted will set you on your own path to a new relationship with your body. *My Pain-Body Solution* is an enjoyable read while serving as a guide to living more fully."

—**Tina Welling,** author of *Writing Wild: Forming a Creative Partnership with Nature*

"If you are suffering from pain and looking for answers, Mike Murray's book, *My Pain-Body Solution*, is a must read. We are lacking patient-centered stories about pain that offer valuable information. As an acupuncturist and pain therapist for ten-plus years, I have dedicated my life to helping those who struggle with difficult pain conditions. This book is both an excellent resource on the current state of mind-body medicine and a trail map for those suffering from unexplained chronic pain."

—**Brendan Carney,** Acupuncture North

"Mike shares his firsthand journey healing from severe pain. If you're looking to understand the deeper roots behind pain and move beyond trauma, this is a great read."

—**Bess O'Connor,** founder and
CEO of Well Spirit Collective

"Much of the chronic and recurrent pain and discomfort that we experience has a psychological basis. This explains why so many continue to suffer despite the best efforts of well-meaning practitioners, whether part of traditional medical fields or alternative ones. Embracing the concepts of mind-body medicine, learning how very real physical symptoms may have a psychological cause, can be life changing. Mike shares his journey to this knowledge with remarkable candor. It's clear that his goal is to help others, and I have no doubt that he will."

—**Marc D. Sopher, M.D.,** author of *To Be or Not To Be . . .
Pain-Free: The Mindbody Syndrome,*
contributor to *The Divided Mind: The Epidemic
of Mindbody Disorders* by John Sarno, M.D.

A JOURNEY *to the*
OTHER SIDE *of* SUFFERING

My
Pain-Body
Solution

MICHAEL J. MURRAY

RIVER GROVE
BOOKS

This book is a memoir reflecting the author's present recollections of experiences over time. Its story and its words are the author's alone. Some details and characteristics may be changed, some events may be compressed, and some dialogue may be recreated.

Published by River Grove Books
Austin, TX
www.rivergrovebooks.com

Distributed by River Grove Books

Design and composition by Greenleaf Book Group
Cover design by Greenleaf Book Group
Cover photo by Michael Murray, Montana Backcountry

Publisher's Cataloging-in-Publication data is available.

Print ISBN: 978-1-63299-454-7

eBook ISBN: 978-1-63299-455-4

First Edition

This book is dedicated to Becky, Mikey, Kaylee, Jaimie, and our four-legged friends, Bernie and Sweet Lou!

Our bodies hold memories of the past. The goal is to access the body memory of the event, not the story, then work to heal and release embodied trauma patterns.

—PETER LEVINE

Contents

PART III: AWAKENING EMOTIONS AND PURPOSE

About the Title

The pain-body is a phrase coined by spiritual teacher Eckhart Tolle. The pain-body is a container of emotional pain stored from the past, carried inside the body. It's an accumulation of difficult experiences that were never fully processed as they happened. We all have a pain-body and it is either dormant or active. It manifests as anger, hurt, hate, anxiety, depression, jealousy, and even physical pain. When active, the pain-body is alive and in control. Its feeds on negative energy of the mind. The solution is to notice the moment the pain-body awakens—catch it then and bring mindful awareness to it.

This has led me to the other side of suffering.

Introduction

This book was written as it was happening, over a span of four years. I wrote it while I was in extreme pain, both physically and, as it turned out, emotionally. I am not a writer, nor have I ever attempted to write a book. I consider myself a *regular guy*. Needless to say, this was a huge undertaking and a challenge for me.

I've learned many lessons along the way. It is my hope as you read these words on the pages that follow that you will be inspired by the teachings I received from the many books I read, the countless podcasts I listened to, the seminars I attended, and the many soulful healers I encountered along the way. Some of this wisdom dates back some 2,500 years.

As you walk with me in Part 1 of this book, you will learn about my seemingly never-ending pattern of pain, the struggles that haunted me, and the interactions I had with the many doctors I consulted with. At times, my tone may come across as harsh or cynical toward many of the medical professionals I met with. Because I wanted to write a true and accurate account, I did not sugarcoat my story. Without a certain level of awareness, these feelings are challenging to navigate when you are in the thick of things, confused and in pain. I experienced ineffective treatments, contradicting diagnoses, and often dispassionate care. But what I have come to understand is that each and every doctor acted with my best interest in mind. They were treating me with the tools at their disposal and what they were taught.

In Part 2, a chance discovery in a book led me to a dawning of awareness of the emotional root of my pain. As I dug deeper into this line of medicine and therapy, I uncovered truths about my past and discovered how protective behaviors I developed along the way caused emotional trauma that was presenting itself as physical and emotional pain for me, at fifty-two years old. The pain would eventually lead me to the other side of suffering, where I began to see what pain was teaching me, and to heal parts of my past that were hidden deep within my consciousness.

The remainder of Part 2 and Part 3 chronicle my healing journey—the type of healing that is readily available to all of us, if we are willing to do the work to uncover the hidden lessons along the way.

No journey is linear and everyone's path is different. In my case, I often took two steps forward and three steps back. Sometimes life is messy. Pain was my teacher and I its unwilling student. Today, however, I view it much differently and, ironically, the pain is practically a distant memory in the rearview mirror of my life.

My wish is that this impacts you and those around you in a positive way. Pain affects each and every one of us.

This is my story.

Michael J. Murray

PART 1:

Searching for Answers

CHAPTER 1

In Pain

As I drove my big red van up Teton Pass under the falling snow, I was still a bit tired from the previous night's flight, the late-night cocktails, and spending time searching the internet for up-to-date information on the incoming storm. In recent years, I had become somewhat obsessed with tracking winter storms that were headed for Wyoming's Teton Range. But there was a reason for my passion.

Skiing powder had become a meaningful part of my life. I had to know the weather patterns, especially since I would be traveling from New Hampshire to Wyoming on short notice to chase these storms. Chasing storms? Sounds ridiculous, right? Not really, not for those who, like me, have discovered the joy in skiing undisturbed snow. I've always been a weather buff and with today's technology, it is easy to track these storms with almost pinpoint accuracy. It's tough to explain, to put into words, the thrill of skiing fresh snow; the experience of skiing deep, virgin powder gives you the sensation of weightlessness—it is really an amazing experience.

I also was fortunate enough to be able to retire eleven years ago at the young age of forty-three, and that's when we purchased a second home at the base of the Teton Range in Jackson Hole, Wyoming, where I was now spending much of my time enjoying the outdoor life—trying to balance being a good father and husband with feeding my ever-growing passions at the same time.

November and December were quickly becoming some of my favorite times to ski the Wyoming Tetons, particularly in the backcountry. The snow always seemed to fall early in this area. Coming from the East Coast where snow was often lacking, it was like a dream, receiving these consistent early-season cold storms rolling down from the Gulf of Alaska, into the Pacific Northwest and finally the Northern Rockies, slamming the impressive Teton Range with copious amounts of early-season powder. The Tetons can cycle up with days, weeks, or even a month of snow. It's something else to experience a long storm cycle. There is no place I would rather be than northwest Wyoming when it's snowing. When I'm out skiing in the backcountry it seems as if nothing else exists or matters.

+ + +

Like others eager to enjoy the early-season snow, I was there on December 4, my first day of the 2016/2017 ski season. Even with the arrival of the storm that should last days, the town and area were empty, as the onslaught of tourists would not show up for another few weeks—it was locals only! The snow was falling heavier as I drove farther up the pass. Each flake that dropped from the sky only added to my burgeoning excitement.

I had opted to ski the backcountry on my first day that season instead of being lift-served at the ski resort. I'd grown to love skiing in the backcountry. There are no ski lifts, so skiing in the backcountry means you have to hike up the mountain in deep snow. You do this by attaching climbing skins to the bottoms of your skis. The skins let you slide your skis forward, but they prevent you from slipping backward as you ascend.

When you reach the top, you peel off your skins before you ski the fresh virgin powder back to the bottom. It's a different experience than skiing from a lift at a resort, but one I enjoy immensely. It's a slower pace, a way to connect with nature as well as rely on yourself, managing the risks of being in the backcountry on your own. There's something about that experience that makes me feel more alive and free. It reminds me of when I was a young boy, walking on my own across the large field by our house into the woods, where I would climb to the very top of a giant tree. With my head, shoulders, and chest exposed to the sky, the branches and limbs seemed to be only as thick as a baseball bat, but apparently thick enough to support my body as I blew with the wind, swaying back and forth fifty feet above the ground. Like skiing in the backcountry, I felt like an adventurer on those days.

I guess that's why I receive so much joy from ski touring; it's a combination of a lot of factors really. There's nothing like being out there having to address your basic needs of eating, staying warm, protecting yourself from the elements, navigating, mitigating avalanche risk, and, of course, pushing yourself physically.

As I continued the drive up the pass and through the massive avalanche path of Glory Bowl, I tried to take a quick peek to my right up into the bowl as I passed through the exposed area while keeping one eye on the road and the anticipated turns ahead. I could hardly contain myself. I swear, if happiness were a pressure cooker, I would have shot right out of my Ford E-250 van. Everywhere I looked, snow blanketed the magnificent terrain. At that moment, I knew it was going to be one hell of season!

There is nothing like starting the ski season with a big storm cycle. The previous year was a breakout winter for me in the backcountry.

After taking an avalanche course and spending many days touring in the backcountry with my son, Mikey, my confidence and comfort levels traveling in avalanche terrain had grown tremendously, and I was looking forward to pushing myself deeper into the backcountry and the sport itself. I had spent the summer and fall poring over maps of the new ski zones in the Wyoming backcountry and was excited about discovering these new areas on my own. I was still a novice, compared to the locals who'd grown up with the Tetons in their backyard, but my passion for the sport was just as strong.

Since it was early in the ski season, my route and skiing that day would be limited to the top half of the peaks, as the snowpack had yet to be established down low. Though I'd be on my own, I was confident I could safely travel in avalanche terrain.

My plan was to park at the top of the pass road, which rises to about 8,500 feet. From there, I would strap my skins on to the bottoms of my skis and tour up for another forty-five minutes to the top of Mount Elly, which rises another 800 feet or so. It was a great early-season powder destination. I didn't think I'd come across anyone either, which was a huge bonus for me.

I was going to take it easy my first day and only ski a couple of laps while I built up my endurance, but I quickly scrapped that plan since the skiing was exceptional and I was feeling strong and motivated. Instead of getting fatigued as the day went on, I found my desire for *one more lap* strengthening with each descent. Touring alone this day did nothing to diminish the joy and excitement I was experiencing. I ended up spending all day skiing powder, a much better day than I'd anticipated, considering this was just the start of the storm cycle that was going to last three or four days. As I headed back to the van and saw the new snow continue to pile up, I was already getting excited about the next day in the backcountry and decided to spend the evening researching new routes to ski.

That evening as the snow continued to drop from the sky and

after an amazing day skiing deep, undisturbed powder, I hoisted my favorite cocktail glass, and my attention was drawn to something on my foot. Before taking a sip of my freshly poured vodka, I took a closer look and noticed I had a decent-sized blister on my right heel. It was probably a bit larger than a quarter. As I studied it, I noticed it was bloodied, raw, and exposed—connected only by a small piece of skin. I continued to study it as I called Becky, my wife of over twenty-five years.

"Hi, Beck," I said when she answered the phone.

"Mike," Becky said, "you made it out in one piece! Thank goodness. I've been waiting for your call. The kids will be thrilled to have you alive for Christmas."

I laughed. "Yes, I'm back safely. It was incredible! I wish you could have been with me. I can't wait till everyone is out here, and I can show you these new zones I've covered. It's amazing and the snow was deep!"

"That's great," she said. "We can't wait to get out there."

"There is something bugging me though," I frowned and leaned closer to my heel. "I have a nasty blister on my foot."

"Oh, I'm sure it's nothing. Put some ointment and a Band-Aid on it. I bet it's gone in a few days."

I supposed she was right and moved on to more exciting topics: the powder on the slopes. "You're going to love it, Beck!"

"Just please try not to get buried in an avalanche. Why don't you call someone to join you? You're in the backcountry, by yourself, no one is around to help you in the event of an emergency—please be safe."

I smiled at her concern. I am fortunate to have a wife who allows me to pursue my passions, even if she worries sometimes. While I know Becky would rather have me home, she understands the enjoyment I get from these trips and is supportive of them.

After our call, I prepared for the next day's tour in the backcountry.

I checked the batteries in my avalanche beacon, made two PB&Js, filled my water bottles, grabbed an energy bar, and powered up my extra phone charger in case of emergency, all in an effort to be ready to go first thing in the morning.

I went to bed early that night and rose before the sun. I adhered to that same schedule for the next nine days: Get up early, ski, go to bed, repeat. There was a certain peace in being organized and keeping things simple, with my singular focus on finding the lightest and deepest snow to ski.

Nine days later, my family started to roll in for the Christmas break. Our son, Mikey, a mechanical engineering major at Montana State University in Bozeman, arrived first. Mikey was followed by our daughter Kaylee, majoring in environmental science at University of Colorado in Boulder. Becky and our youngest daughter, Jaimie, an eighth grader, were the last to arrive. It was great to have the family together. Since we'd purchased our condo in Wyoming, it had become a tradition to spend Christmas there.

Besides a trivial squabble here or there, the five of us get along and truly enjoy each other's company. We love our time in Jackson together.

A few days after Christmas, while we all skied at the resort, I noticed what I thought might be a small hamstring pull. It didn't feel too bad, just very tight, but when you're fifty-two years old, how could any hamstring pull be good? Unlike when I was younger, almost everything took longer to heal. I'd planned to stay and tour the backcountry once the rest of the family returned home, but the hamstring issue had me concerned. Could I even do that now? In the days leading up to the New Year, I skied with everyone, but I held back from letting my skis really "run" and kept them on the snow versus getting in the air, avoiding the usual risks. Every time I was alone, however, I wondered, "How do I get this hamstring thing to just go away?"

After my family left, I was still able to ski, but hiking in the rugged wilderness was painful. It was not debilitating, but it hurt. Often, a mild tearing sensation in the back of my thigh would be followed by tenderness in a few hours. I used most of my downtime trying to figure out when I'd injured the muscle and how I could speed up the healing, rotating between icing it and applying heat each evening. I ultimately cut my stay short and headed back to New Hampshire to rest in the hope that I would recover in time for a major ski trip I'd planned with Mikey.

This injury had me worried. I only had two months until our big Alaskan skiing adventure, and I needed to be healthy.

+ + +

When I returned home to the New Hampshire seacoast, I felt like a defeated man. Though my hamstring pain wasn't that bad, it had been a long time since I'd pulled a muscle, and I was worried this could take months to heal. And the clock was ticking for me, Mikey, and Alaska.

In our beautiful New England seacoast town, I decided to take it easy and rest. It was not snowing in Wyoming right then, so I hadn't missed a single storm cycle, which I found comforting.

As active as I like to be, I'm also quite capable of sitting on the couch for a couple of days doing nothing. But on day three, the surf swell appeared. It wasn't huge, but it was big enough to get me excited—maybe waist- to chest-high waves, with winds coming out of the west, which should make ideal surfing conditions, right outside our front door.

I'd transitioned to stand-up paddleboarding (SUP) in the last year or so, because I had both shoulders operated on eight years prior as a result of arthritis and bone spurs. SUP surfing is much easier on my shoulders versus traditional prone surfing, which required my arms to be extended above my head. A little over two years after I retired in 2010, I remember putting on my ski shell and feeling a sharp pain in my left shoulder as I pushed my arm through the sleeve. I'd never had shoulder problems before. I was an avid tennis player, I surfed, and I even threw batting practice during Mikey's baseball season.

That's what got me—pain had never been an issue. But I developed a sharp pain that haunted me all that summer, even after I saw a doctor who got me into physical therapy and administered two cortisone shots. Later that summer, the same issue happened with my right shoulder. This forced me to give up tennis, surfing, and biking. I could not do anything. I ultimately had surgery that allowed me to become active again.

Becky and I surfed for a couple of hours and had a great time enjoying the cold winter waves together. Once I got home and took off my thick 5mm wetsuit, I did a quick stretch and felt confident that I had not harmed my sore hamstring. Normally after surfing, cycling, or skiing I'd be in a really good mood. But that day was different. Something was off. Though the pain in the hamstring was mild, I was overly preoccupied with it, and that was preventing me from enjoying the afterglow of the surf session. If things didn't improve, I might need to set up an appointment with my doctor, just to make sure everything was OK.

The next morning as I was drinking coffee, I noticed a sharp pain in my left shoulder. I told Becky about this, and she assured me I must have slept on it wrong. With yesterday's surf session still fresh in my mind and recognizing I'd had no unusual fall that could have tweaked my shoulder, I accepted Becky's explanation of sleeping the wrong way. But concerns resurfaced because of my prior shoulder problems and the suppressed fear that had begun with those surgeries eight years ago.

Days after the first shoulder surgery, while in physical therapy (PT), my therapist made a passing comment about working with shoulder replacement patients. That small remark stuck with me. From that day forward, I believed that shoulder replacement was my ultimate fate, regardless of whether that was true or not. This dread weighed heavily on my mind. Apparently, I was a worst-case-scenario patient.

But now, as the end of January approached, my hamstring and shoulder were both in dire straits. To make matters worse, Alaska was having a historically bad winter. While Mikey's and my trip was not until the end of March, I knew it needed to start snowing there soon or that trip would be a bust. I was filled with anxiety thinking of the possibility of things not working out for Mikey and me in Alaska. I wanted so badly for him to have an amazing experience. We both had the same fire in our bellies for skiing.

I now spent my days resting my hamstring and shoulder, while tracking the storms that were getting diverted from Alaska and pushed south into the Pacific Northwest and then the Northern Rockies. I didn't speak to anyone about my internal struggles, negative thoughts, or fears. In retrospect, I probably should have.

At the end of January, which felt like an eternity to me, I finally saw a doctor for my hamstring. I had wanted to see a doctor weeks earlier, but since the pain was not that bad, I'd hoped rest would heal it. The doctor did not take any images, feeling rest and physical therapy should do the trick. The doctor was very confident I would be ready for my Alaska trip in March. I left the appointment with some relief, but again, down deep were these lingering doubts and fears I just couldn't shake. It's hard to explain, but it was like I constantly felt frozen in fear, and I just couldn't move beyond that feeling.

Over the next couple of weeks, I got a better handle on my injuries; not that they'd improved, but I became more confident I could move with them. My hamstring seemed to bother me more sitting down than standing up and moving around, and my left shoulder only hurt when I tried to reach behind me. So I simply avoided those movements as much as possible. This solution wasn't ideal, yet nothing would stop me from skiing. But dammit, it still wasn't snowing in Alaska!

The last week of February, Jaimie had her school break. We'd invited one of her good friends, Mia, and Mia's father, Dan, a good friend of ours, to Wyoming.

The ski conditions were great at the resort, and skiing with Jaimie and Mia always put a smile on my face. I loved watching them laugh and goof around. After struggling the past two months and not having much fun in my life, I had definite moments of joy during their visit. But one afternoon, after a great day of skiing, we came back to our condo, and something set me off. Perhaps it was the presence of my constant nagging injuries or maybe I took another disheartening look at the Alaska weather patterns. Maybe I'll never know, but something came over me and all I could do was retreat to my bedroom to avoid Jaimie, Mia, and Dan.

I was overcome with emotions and didn't want anyone to know. Tears began welling up in my eyes. I'd been really wound up the last two months because of my injuries and the lack of snow in Alaska, but crying was something entirely new for me.

Becky walked into the bedroom and asked, "What's going on? Are you OK?"

My head was buried in some blankets on the bed so she couldn't tell I was crying. I pulled my head out and said, "I don't know what's wrong with me. I feel terrible, and I just can't face those guys."

"Are you sick?" Becky asked.

I shook my head and wiped the tears. Becky sat on the bed next to me, looking at me with confusion. She was probably in shock to see me crying. This breakdown should have been a clue that something bigger was going on with me emotionally. Why was I crying over poor snow conditions and a couple of minor injuries? How could I not see how fortunate I was to be here, at the doorstep of the

Teton Range with my family and dear friends? Becky recognized I needed some time to pull myself together and offered to go pick up some pizza.

I saw the worry in her eyes as she left.

CHAPTER 2

Dark and Alone

A s feared, the conditions in Alaska did not work out. But Mikey and I had a great time being in a remote part of the state and enjoying the beauty of the mountains. Once we landed back in Bozeman and I said goodbye to Mikey at the college, I started my four-hour drive back to Jackson Hole. It's a drive I usually love to take because I'm either cruising north in the red van to Bozeman to hang out with Mikey and ski or fly-fish or I'm in the van heading south back to Jackson Hole to ski or fly-fish. You get the drift. As a couple of friends like to say about me, I'm a "fun-hog on the move!"

This ride, however, was different. I was tired and ready to go home. I don't think I even played music on the drive back. Instead, I just kept shifting my weight in the seat to alleviate the pressure on my hamstring.

When I got home from the Alaska trip, my shoulder was still in pain, so I decided to have it evaluated by the same doctor who'd performed surgery on both of my shoulders eight years before. I arrived at that appointment fifteen minutes early and sat quietly, trying not to call attention to myself in case that led to a conversation with a friendly stranger—*God forbid*. Lately, I found myself more comfortable not talking to anyone. I just wanted to be left alone with my pain and anxiety.

After a nurse took an X-ray of my shoulder, she escorted me to an exam room, where I waited for the images and the doctor's arrival.

When the doctor walked in, we exchanged pleasantries. He examined my shoulders and seemed somewhat satisfied with my range of motion and the lack of scar tissue from his handiwork years earlier. He then looked at the X-ray and nodded.

"Do you think the arthritis has progressed? Is that why I'm feeling this pain?" I asked, frowning.

He toggled back and forth between that day's image and the image taken eight years ago.

"The arthritis hasn't progressed. I'd just get some rest and do some PT. I'll write you a script for physical therapy twice a week for six weeks. That should do it."

It was a massive relief to hear the arthritis had not worsened. This instantly lightened my mental load. Wow, I wouldn't need a shoulder replacement after all.

While he was writing the script, he turned to me and asked, "How's your other shoulder been?"

"Fine. Really. But my hamstring is a mess," I said, rubbing the back of my right leg. "I just can't seem to shake it."

The doctor studied me for a moment. "Why don't we get some X-rays to see what's going on?"

I knew he was more of a shoulder specialist, but my hamstring was killing me, so I agreed. After about twenty minutes of waiting for the leg X-ray, I was escorted back to the same exam room. I sat quietly and watched as the doctor grabbed the image from the counter and held it up to the light.

Without any hesitation, he proclaimed, "You've got arthritis in the hip. A hip replacement would work well here."

Wait, what? I'd known down deep the last three months that something was very wrong, but a hip replacement?

"Excuse me?" was all I could muster, as I sat there completely floored.

My eyes were tearing, so he quickly shifted gears and asked me to hop up on the exam table.

"Point to where you're feeling the pain," he said. "What activities make it worse?"

Without thinking, I said, "Sitting? Sitting makes it worse."

At the time it made no sense why I was in more pain when idle, but it was true. I also tried to explain a move called a *kick turn* while skinning up in steep terrain that was becoming difficult.

While I shared my list, he manipulated my right hip and leg.

"Hmmm . . . I think we need to do an MRI. These symptoms don't sound like an arthritic hip."

An MRI? I began to worry, as was my nature, but only nodded, knowing that whatever the problem was, I wanted relief. Soon after, I was taken to get an MRI, but the results would not be back until the next day.

I ran into the doctor in the hallway on my way out and couldn't even muster the strength to speak.

"I'll call you in the next day or so," he said with a kind smile, "once I've had a chance to look over the imaging."

I nodded and then walked as fast as I could out of his office, as I could feel the tears welling up. Once in my car, I sat in silence, staring at the dash. Aware of nothing but the dark cloud that surrounded me, my breathing became heavy.

Then my thoughts—and heart—began to race. Would I need a hip replacement? How does that even work? What would happen to my skiing, cycling, surfing? Could I still do all of that? I wasn't even sure what they would replace. But I was sure that life as I knew it would be over.

Before pulling out of the parking lot, I tried to call Becky, but she didn't pick up. So I called my oldest brother, John, who had experience in the medical field.

While trying to catch my breath, I explained the situation. It couldn't have been easy for him to listen to his fifty-two-year-old younger brother cry. We talked for ten minutes but all I remember him saying was, "You want to put off a hip replacement as long as possible. It's a hell of a procedure."

I know he meant well, but that was the last thing I needed to hear. What I heard him tell me was that a hip replacement was so bad, I was better off living in pain than getting it done.

Shit, that's bad . . . really bad. Fear took over. I literally couldn't move. I sat in my car for several minutes before I was ready to head home.

How was it that I was skiing the Alaska backcountry two weeks ago with no issue other than a small hamstring pull and now I needed a hip replacement? If only I'd asked the doctor that question.

Days later, while I was driving, my phone rang. My first reaction was to let it go to voicemail, as I was in no mood to speak to anyone. But the number was unknown, and I thought maybe it was my doctor calling with the MRI results. I answered the phone, and it was him. He told me he had the results. After looking over the film, he reversed course and believed the pain was actually coming from tendinitis of the hamstring. In addition to the PT script he'd written for my shoulder, he would write one for my hamstring, too. *Thank God.* I felt as if I had just dodged a speeding bullet. Instantly, strong emotions of happiness and joy enveloped me. To keep with this feeling, I quickly thanked him for the call and said goodbye, purposely not asking any questions about the arthritis in my right hip.

Out of sight, out of mind, right? On the car ride home, I had the windows down, my fingers tapping the steering wheel, singing like Tom Cruise in *Jerry Maguire* to Tom Petty's "Free Fallin'." I was so happy. If only I could bottle that sensation! How could I go from despair to jubilation in seconds? Could a doctor's message hold that much power over me?

Within two weeks of hearing my doctor tell me that he believed the pain was a result of tendinitis, I found myself at my first physical therapy session. I was assigned to a young, athletic therapist named Julie. She didn't try to impress me with facts and information. She wanted to know about me and my pain. "I know what it's like to be on the sidelines," she said. "I like to cycle as well, and I have had plenty of injuries too that prevented me from being active. I get it, I do, Mike." There was an overcall calmness to her that made me feel relaxed, which allowed me to immediately open up to her. I felt very comfortable talking with her. While my anxiety had improved a bit the past week, I think she picked up on how I was feeling, so she did not leave my side. I felt safe and comfortable with her, sensing I was in good hands. We talked about my left shoulder and right hamstring.

"Which injury would you like to start with?" she asked.

Seeing as how I had been given a new lease on the hip without getting a new hip, I said, "The shoulder."

We had a good session as Julie put me through some easy stretches for my shoulder and finished by applying some warm heat. It felt like my shoulder was already getting better by the time I walked out of my first appointment.

Two days later, I'd gotten Julie's approval for an easy bike ride. My plan was to ride a manageable fifteen miles. While I had felt better at PT, I was still feeling off. I had been pacing around all morning, impatiently trying to find all my bike gear. My mouth had been dry, I was tense, and I had to drink a ton of water before I even got on the bike. I decided to keep the ride under the radar and not alert Becky. Looking back, I see that I had little confidence that the ride would be a success, and while the physical pain had me concerned, I now know it was emotional angst that was the bigger issue. And as I would learn in the years ahead, communicating when I was struggling was not something that came naturally to me.

However, while sneaking down the back staircase, Becky saw me in my spandex riding gear. I froze on the steps as a smile came over her face.

"You're getting back on your bike!" she said. I thought for a moment she would clap her hands together and start a cheer.

I shrugged and gave her a half-hearted grin. Truth be told, I was anything but excited. My nerves had taken over. I was afraid the pain would increase. I'd been in agony for over four months now, and I hated it.

Patience had never been my strong suit.

I was no more than a hundred yards out of our driveway when my left shoulder started to throb with pain anytime I hit a small imperfection in the road. About halfway through the ride, the pain from my shoulder had crept into my neck, which limited my ability to look over my left shoulder. My ride and fate almost ended abruptly in a collision with a car coming from behind as I pulled an unexpected U-turn without being able to look over my left shoulder. I needed to get home—if only I weren't on that damn bike. At least my hamstring wasn't bugging me. Glass half full? I struggled to bike home, and of course, about an hour and a half after the ride, my right glute and right hip bone started to hurt with a sharp, radiating pain.

As much as I'd wished otherwise, it was now clear to me that road biking would not be part of my rehabilitation. So I started to spend the bulk of each day in our little fitness room stretching and performing some easy range-of-motion exercises. It was also a good way to spend time away from people. With my increasing anxiety and approaching depression, I perceived social interactions as uncomfortable and likely leading to greater suffering. And I desperately wanted to avoid that. The last thing I needed was more discomfort.

Deciding I couldn't bike, I started walking daily. I'd always been bored with walking. But now I had no choice. During my walks, I could feel new pain surfacing in my right glute and the side and front of my right hip. It was a peculiar sensation. The bone pain seemed to move around. It was there one second, gone the next. Though my doctor had said it was tendinitis of the hamstring, all these new pains had me thinking about the arthritis and the questions I'd neglected to ask.

As time went on, I found myself becoming more and more isolated. My life, at least the last ten years, since I'd retired, had revolved around my passions: cycling, surfing, hiking, fly-fishing, and skiing. I couldn't do any of those things now, so what did I have to offer friends and family? What could we even talk about? Of course, now I realize I am much more than my hobbies. I have since discovered a depth I never knew because of my pain-journey. But then, well . . . I was a man made up only of outdoor adventure, or so I thought. I also came to a new realization. I'd always thought I had a high threshold for pain. It turned out that that couldn't have been further from the truth. I hated pain! The high tolerance I *thought* I had was actually me ignoring the discomfort and its meaning.

For the next month, my typical day would consist of three sessions of stretching, each stint lasting about forty-five minutes. I would then spend another fifteen minutes or so lying on the mat with my iPhone inches from my face, googling my various injuries. I was determined to find what ailed me. I do *not* recommend this course of action. Dr. Google will only slowly drive you insane while making you believe certain death is imminent.

During my walks, I became constantly aware of the pains in my body. I decided to start keeping a detailed log. I recorded each stretch session, the distance walked, and my pain scale throughout the day. And while this "pain log" could be depressing with its daily entries, it was one of the best things I could have done. It allowed me to slowly start to share and experience my emotions.

I was now letting all my calls go directly to voicemail—*who had the energy or desire to actually speak to people?*—and I returned each with a text message and a lame-ass excuse as to why I couldn't talk.

One sunny afternoon, Becky found me in the fitness room, the blinds drawn, lying on my mat in total darkness. Again. For the past month or so, I'd been spending at least three to four hours a day in this room. In this position. Alone.

"Mike."

I blinked open my eyes at the sound of Becky's concerned voice.

"Hmm?"

"Are you coming out?" she asked. "I'm taking the dogs on a walk. Maybe you can join us this time? Jaimie is coming too."

Staring at the ceiling, I shrugged.

"I know Jaimie would like to do something with you," Becky said. "And *I'm* worried."

"Everything's fine." Maybe if I said it often enough, I thought, it would become the truth, and I could be left alone.

"You can't just lie here all day," Becky said. "Have you spoken to Mikey and Kaylee lately? They said you haven't returned their calls. Why don't you get in touch with them?"

"I will. I'm just trying to relax."

"Mike . . . this isn't helping."

I could hear the sadness in my wife's voice. I didn't like my behavior at all, but I couldn't stop. At the time, I didn't think I deserved to be happy, and I began to sink deeper. Looking back now, it's hard to recall how I isolated myself like that. It is as if I were a different person who was unrecognizable. Because now I see how valuable simple human connection is—whether it is a walk in nature with my kids, a quick chat with a friend, or sharing a tidbit of my day with Becky—all those moments matter and add up. I had no idea of the depths that I had let myself fall to.

The only thing that helped was PT with Julie. She was so reassuring, and she listened to me. We developed a bond and shared a love for cycling. During PT, we talked about our shared passion for hill climbs while cycling.

"Last year I climbed the Kancamagus Highway in the White Mountains," I told her. "I started in Conway and finished with the descent into Lincoln. The final push is a killer but so spectacular!"

"I know that exact spot!" Julie said. "I've ridden that road so many times, but always in the opposite direction! Gorgeous in the fall!" She asked what other big climbs I'd recommend.

She seemed wholeheartedly engaged in our conversation, as well as the treatment, so I found it easy to open up to her.

"I'm really scared that I have significant arthritis in my hip and both shoulders," I said. "I toss and turn every night worrying about having to replace these joints."

Julie calmly replied, "Granted, I haven't seen the images, but from what I can tell after working with you is the arthritis is not causing the pain and you won't need joint replacements. I *will* get you back in the game. You'll be climbing up the 'Kanc' again before you know it!" She gave me a huge grin.

Leaving each session with Julie always filled me with a renewed sense of hope, as well as some actual relief from my physical pain. I now see because I respected and trusted her—and most important, because she was engaged and listened to me—I was able to let my guard down and relax. Unfortunately, those moments of relief were always short-lived, despite what I thought at the time were my best efforts to remain positive.

The reality of the situation was that I provided little effort to resist the anxiety and depression that inevitably would creep back in. I just went with where my emotions took me. It simply seemed easier to give in to my emotions than disrupt them.

CHAPTER 3

Taking Control

Even though the doctor said my shoulder was fine and no surgery was needed, did it really matter? I was still in horrible pain, and it had been four months with no lasting improvement. And while I wanted to believe Julie when she said arthritis was not the cause of my pain, I still had my doubts. I felt I needed to do more, so I sought another opinion.

Becky, who was equally eager to get me feeling better, was able to arrange two doctor appointments for me through an acquaintance of hers. The first would be with an orthopedic shoulder specialist; the second would be with his partner, who was a hip specialist, but that would be four weeks later.

The day before I would meet the shoulder specialist, I was at one of Jaimie's lacrosse games with Becky and a friend of ours. As we stood by the bleachers, I bent down to tie my sneakers and felt as if my whole body locked up. I could not reach my shoes. I was in excruciating pain; my back—from my waist to my shoulders—felt as if it were in a viselike grip, preventing me from moving in a vertical direction. I casually walked away from them, my heart racing, in search of a large rock or picnic table to place my foot on. When I returned, my face was hot and I worried if everyone noticed that my shoes were still untied.

Now, in addition to the huge pain from this vise grip, there was the great embarrassment I felt trying to hide my untied shoes from the other parents. I had no interest in revealing my pain, finding it difficult to share my weaknesses. What was happening? Why did my back pain suddenly spike? In my mind, I kept coming back to the imaging I had seen of my deteriorated hip. Was it arthritis after all? Was the initial diagnosis correct?

The next day I drove to the shoulder specialist appointment by myself. In hindsight, I should have brought someone with me. It was a huge struggle just to get in and out of the car with my hip, shoulder, and now back pain. I hung my head and slogged toward the building. *Would this ever freaking end?*

I made it into the exam room and the specialist eventually walked in with the month-old images I had FedExed to his office. I was expecting him to comment on them, but he simply looked at me and said, "The arthritis in your shoulder looks mild. Let's try some PT."

I nodded. Same as the last shoulder guy said.

The doctor added, "I could also go in and clean it up, remove some of the bone spurs, if you want. That might help." He didn't seem very confident about that statement.

"However, you should put off a shoulder replacement as long as you can."

In my worst-case scenario, Dr. Google-mind again led me to hear this and assume a shoulder replacement was inevitable.

Hey, maybe a replacement won't be that bad if—

"You just can't do that much once you have a shoulder replaced," he continued.

Great. Here we go again.

He then pulled up the MRI of my hip. I was seeing his partner, the hip specialist, in a few weeks, but he wanted to tell me what he saw in the image and what his partner might suggest.

"Your hips are in bad shape."

Yeah, I've heard, doc.

"You'll definitely need to replace them."

My shoulders sagged.

Studying my disappointment, he added, "I had my hip replaced a few years ago, and my X-ray looked just like this."

I didn't respond.

"It's really not that bad. Unlike shoulder replacement, hip replacements are pretty amazing, and you can be very active if you're good about your PT and wait until you're fully recovered before hitting the slopes again."

Tears started rolling down my cheeks. Since the onset of the hamstring and shoulder pain, I had become accustomed to crying.

The doctor patted me on the shoulder. "You know what? After my hip replacement, I had my best ski season ever."

Looking back, I know he was simply trying to pick up my spirits, but his words had the opposite effect.

The drive home was nerve-wracking. Now I had a hip that needed to be replaced, and the only answer for my agonizing shoulder was "hold off on shoulder replacement as long as you can."

Which means living with the agonizing pain as long as I can!
SHIT. SHIT. SHIT.

I called Becky.

"Hi, Beck," I said with a sigh.

"What did the doctor say?"

"Apparently, I need a full body replacement."

"What? Mike, what did he really—?"

"Look, I'll fill you in later. I need to go."

As soon as Becky had picked up the phone, I'd realized I just wanted to be by myself. I drove home on autopilot and in a fog, replaying in my head what the doctor had told me. That night I had trouble sleeping. I kept thinking about the hip replacement, even though I had not seen the hip specialist yet. I was also worried that my shoulder was going to fail me too. It felt like my entire body was falling apart!

The next day I tried to stay positive while I resumed my stretching in our dark, small workout room. What was amazing is all the stretching I'd been doing had not seemed to help at all. In spite of that, I gave myself a pep talk: "Stay positive, Mike. Just take this one day at a time. You have a great, loving family."

I'd like to say that all that self-talk helped. But it did not. All the talk about joint replacements and what it meant to my lifestyle was starting to take a toll on me in odd ways. The evening after the appointment, I went to the mall with Becky to pick up some birthday presents for Jaimie and Kaylee. They were born on the same date, April 30, five years apart.

Within minutes of entering the mall, my vision became tunnel-like and everything began closing in on me. The air was warm to my skin, and I heard a small humming sound coming from the ceiling. My breathing turned shallow as I was hit with a massive wave of anxiety and fear. I was in a nightmare, worse than anything I'd ever experienced. As Becky meandered through each of the stores, I trailed behind her, unsure of what to do except keep breathing. Not fully understanding what was happening, I was aware enough to hide what I was experiencing from Becky and simply tried to hold on. I still lacked the ability to be open when I struggled. I was scared but had no idea why. Losing control in a public place was horrifying.

Uncomfortable by Becky's side and not able to understand or express to her what was going on, I staggered out of a store to the middle of the mall and collapsed onto a bench. People filed past me, though I felt as if I was in a different dimension, invisible to most. I felt isolated, like I was having a nightmare, except I was wide awake. The physical pain in my back and shoulder was there, but the intense fear I experienced was unbearable. It was unrelenting.

I somehow made it to the car with Becky without revealing my panicked state—surely an Academy Award–winning feat—and on the drive home I finally gathered the courage to confess to Becky what I was experiencing, including my fears.

"I just want to be happy, Beck," I said, the dam finally bursting. "I don't care about skiing, hiking, or biking, I just want to be happy again." I was shocked I was able to utter those words. I knew I was in bad shape.

She put her hand gently on mine. "Everything is going to be OK. I'll be here for you . . . always."

I knew at this point that Becky realized my problems extended well beyond chronic physical pain into an emotional realm, a place neither of us had yet explored. This was something we hadn't had a chance to discuss because there simply wasn't time to process and understand it. My pain and emotions went from one crisis to the next, and I'm sure Becky was just trying to keep the ship upright— for me and our kids—by consoling me, assuring me time and again that we would get through this.

I woke up late the next morning, silently thanking Becky for allowing me to sleep in. As I lay in bed, I took inventory of my physical pain and I noticed how I was doing emotionally. Surprisingly, I felt calm. As the morning crawled along, I felt the anxiety wanting to creep back in, but I was able to keep it at bay. Not that I had tools at this point to manage my emotions. I was like a flag in the wind. Whatever direction the wind blew was where I went.

The previous night's episode at the mall had scared me and I didn't want to experience that ever again. I started to recognize that the isolation route I had chosen probably was not helping, and I knew I needed to try something different. I reached out to a good friend a few days later to see if he wanted to have coffee. Over the years, Carl and I would talk or text on a regular basis. But with my radio silence these past few months, he knew something was up; he just wasn't sure what it was.

I arrived at Carl's house with coffee in hand, and we sat and relaxed on the stools at his kitchen bar.

"I've been under water," I began after a few minutes of silence.

"What's going on, man?" Carl asked. "I haven't heard from you in ages."

I sighed. "I'm in constant pain. My shoulder, my hip. The doctors are talking about replacements. But not yet. Of course not . . . don't do anything yet. Just live in agony."

"I didn't know it was that bad," Carl said.

"I spend eighty percent of my waking hours thinking about my pain."

Carl frowned and looked suitably disturbed by my comment. In my mind, I admitted it was more like ninety-five percent. But I kept that to myself, seeing Carl's reaction.

"The worst is that no one can help me *now*," I continued. "I don't want to be a burden, so I've just been holing up. Isolating for months. Dealing with it the best I can." I felt the tears well up and brushed them away, hoping to hide them from Carl.

"You need to let Becky in," Carl said. "There's no reason to be alone with this. And you know I am always here for you, just as I know you would be for me."

"But—"

"And keep trying to find some answers. Don't settle for what those doctors have told you. You can't live in pain."

"Well, if I don't listen to the experts . . ."

"They don't know everything. In the meantime, lean on your family. Your friends. We're here for you, man."

The idea that medical doctors might not have all the answers hadn't dawned on me. I wasn't ready yet to embrace this concept.

"Thanks, Carl. Even talking about how hard it's been helps."

"Cool. But let's do beer next time."

I smiled. "Deal."

"Hey, before you leave, I've got a book you might like. I haven't read it, but another good friend who has a lot pain from spinal issues swears by it. Says it really helped him. I'll get a copy and drop it in your mailbox."

"That sounds great, Carl, thank you."

I felt a million times better when I left Carl's house, and for the first time in months, I actually jammed to some music on the car ride home: "Blaze On" by Phish. Carl had provided some good support, though I had zero interest in reading a book on managing my pain. Unfortunately, the buoyant feeling from the visit didn't last long. Soon, the pain increased again and so did my isolation.

In addition to my seclusion and constant stretching to try to alleviate the pain, I was now taking a lot of warm showers. Up to five a day. There did not appear to be any lasting positive effects from these showers, but they gave me a sense of security in the enclosed space and comfort from the warm water that hit my body. I may have been a mess emotionally and physically, but I was one clean cat!

+ + +

While waiting for my appointment with the hip surgeon, I got an appointment with a *different* hip specialist, who had come highly recommended, on the North Shore of Boston, about an hour away from our home. I wanted to get another opinion and told him my story, of how my pain started with the hamstring, went to the glutes, then the lower back. And how I'd recently developed knee pain out of the blue after I rolled out of bed one morning. He nodded as if he'd heard this story a thousand times. He had the X-ray and MRI that I had had done a month ago. He was critical of the fact that they did an MRI. He said if I'd come to him first, he would not have made that decision.

He proceeded to push my right knee toward my left knee. I instantly grimaced in pain.

"See," he said, "that's all I need to know."

His "I'm smarter than everyone else" attitude rubbed me the wrong way, but I gave him a pass. I was desperate and wanted a solution. Of course, looking back, this impulsive attitude of blindly accepting the explanations of my various doctors had gotten me nowhere fast.

He told me my right hip would need to be replaced and my left hip was one or two years behind that.

Yeah, I'd heard it all before, even though the second hip was a new wrinkle.

"Take your time," the doctor said. "You don't have to schedule the procedure now. You won't damage them further. I just want you to be prepared."

Prepared. Was that a good thing or a bad thing? I guess it was good to put everything out on the proverbial table. But then *it's out there.* You can't take it back. And while you're waiting, there's ample time to worry and second-guess and dread. I had mastered each of those things.

The doctor was waiting for me to respond, so instead of making the decision myself, I again looked to the medical community to make it for me and asked, "What would you do if you were me?"

He smiled. "I would have it replaced."

As I thought it over, dread began to seep in, but in an odd way, there was also a bit of relief, because I finally had my answer. It had been almost five months of pain; all the stretching, PT, and warm showers weren't helping. I didn't know much about joint replacements, so I assumed if the joints were the cause of my pain, there would be no hope of improving until I had them replaced. It would be a continuous downward spiral. As it was, I could no longer put on socks or shoes without sitting down and even that was painful. And walking any distance had becoming increasingly slow and difficult.

It was hard to believe that less than six weeks before the appointment, I had been with Mikey skiing in the Chugach range of Alaska. I was getting worse, and I was looking for someone to take control and provide a definitive answer to my problem. So, for better or worse, we canceled the appointment with the hip surgeon I'd not yet seen and scheduled the surgery with this new specialist. After all, he was positive about the surgery and what I would be able to do athletically once I finished my rehab. His smile was friendly and, at the time, his bedside manner was comforting. Waiting for a second opinion just felt like I would be dragging out the inevitable. There really was no decision as to whether I should do it. I was in terrible pain and was told this would take care of it. I was offered no other option.

This is a regret I live with. The surgeon with whom I canceled would have injected my hip with some sort of substance. Over the course of a month or so, this injection, I was told, would confirm the source of the pain. But I dreaded the thought of "waiting" another month to confirm the source. I was far too impatient and scheduled the surgery with a doctor who didn't require the time-consuming injection procedure. So many regrets.

Leading up to the surgery, which would happen in three weeks, I continued to work with Julie in PT. We agreed all our time would now be spent working on my shoulder, since I would be getting a new hip. Over the next few weeks, I continued to struggle with shooting pains that would come at any time in both glutes, both shoulders, my lower back, neck, and both knees. It seemed my bad hip had my whole body out of alignment. Each morning, I would wake up hoping the pain would be gone. Some mornings it would be, only to come back by midday. I continued searching for answers to the problems beyond my hip, still somehow believing I would find them on the internet!

My knees were swollen and ached. Would I need four joint replacements? Both hips and both knees? Was I stretching *too* much? Was that even possible? Or was it something else? Something worse? And what about my shoulder? Maybe it would be six replacements! I have since learned my behavior was called *catastrophizing*, which is when you assume the worst will happen to you. I wished I knew how to stop; to slow down, take some deep breaths, and relax. I now know with complete certainty that pain is made worse when you worry or catastrophize. According to Katie Sandler, a mental health counselor, "People who cope with various types of stress, anxiety, depression, PTSD, pain issues, and obsessive-compulsive disorder tend to experience catastrophic thinking far more often than those who don't."[1]

Growing up, I can't remember having physical, fear-based obsessions. In fact, I had no fear jumping off high rocks at swimming holes or pulling crazy stunts on skis. I was never afraid of hurting myself, yet now I couldn't control this negative thinking.

In addition to my hours of stretching, PT with Julie, and countless warm showers, I'd begun asking Becky to massage my neck every day. I'd followed Carl's advice and had asked her for help. And while the physical relief was short-lived, I received much-needed emotional relief through her touch and soft voice. I was amazed by her willingness to massage my neck on demand. *If only I could be so kind.* Perhaps this was a window into my shortcomings. Why was I not as giving?

---

1   Everygirl, "How to Tell If Your Mind Suffers from 'Catastrophizing,'" by Kim Quindlen, October 28, 2018, https://theeverygirl.com/catastrophizing/.

CHAPTER 4

Hip Replacement

On May 22, 2017, Becky and I made our way to the hospital. By now, this was old hat for me. I had undergone four surgeries in the past ten years: one to repair my ACL; then arthroscopic surgeries on both shoulders; and there was that plate that was inserted in my finger after I'd crushed it in a skiing accident. While I'd always been nervous going under the knife, I always had a sense of optimism heading in. But this morning was different. I felt empty. Though I tried to make myself believe this procedure would work, I couldn't believe that a new hip would eliminate all the pain I had in my shoulders, neck, glutes, and knees. I mean, how could it?

As the anesthesiologist told me to count backwards, I tried to remember the song my kids used to sing in elementary school: "The thigh bone's connected to the . . . hip bone. The hip bone's connected to the back bone . . ." *But was the back bone connected to the knee bone?*

After what seemed like only moments later, I woke up in the

recovery room, groggy from the anesthesia. I had some tightness in my groin, but all in all, I felt fairly comfortable. As I lay there with my eyes closed, I could hear my doctor making his rounds.

When he entered my room, I opened my eyes. He was all smiles. "Things went great. I lengthened your leg during the procedure."

I nodded, processing what he was telling me—was part of the original plan to lengthen my leg? Did I even need a longer leg? Completely thrown, it was hard for me to tell if the news was good or bad.

Before I could ask, he said, "Your other hip is a little worse than I thought, so we're probably going to have to replace it in the next two to four months."

Still dazed, I didn't have the energy or guts to ask him what happened to the one to two years he had suggested when we first met less than five weeks ago. Had he taken a peek inside my left hip once he had my right hip opened up? Weren't joint replacements based on pain? How would he know that I would be in pain on my left side in two to four months? I had no pain now.

What little spirit I had left had just been taken from me. In spite of my skepticism, the doctor seemed pretty damn happy about it all. I could not believe those were some of the first words out of his mouth after surgery. *Good news! More surgery!*

I then wondered if this was why he'd lengthened my leg, in preparation for his next surgery on me. With my warped thought process, cynical nature, and nonsensical reasoning, I believed he would need to make sure both legs matched in length. So, he took care of the right side first. Like I said, it makes no sense now, but at the time, my reasoning was flawless. Before the doctor left my room, I told him, still in a fog, that my knees had been bothering me before this surgery.

He nodded and said, "Well, those pains should go away in a week or so."

This wasn't much comfort. In fact, it sounded like he was

saying, "If your pain doesn't go away in a week or so, you're pretty much fucked."

"My anxiety is also skyrocketing."

He smiled at me with condescension. "You probably need to relax."

The first few days after surgery went well. I could move around with a cane, and I was cautiously optimistic about how my body was feeling. *Could a new hip really affect everything else so quickly?* This was encouraging. Maybe I wouldn't need knee replacement after all! Or another hip replacement. Or new shoulders!

Before I resumed working with Julie, I had home PT visits. During the first home appointment two days after surgery, I told the visiting nurse I was feeling pretty good and that my knees no longer bothered me.

She quickly said, "Oh yeah, that's the effect of the spinal tap. It will wear off."

"Of course it will," I mumbled in disgust.

During my second home appointment, as I slowly made my way downstairs, I overheard Becky say to the nurse, "Mike is really nervous he is going to need a knee replacement."

When I walked into the room, the nurse told me it was very normal to have knee pain before and after hip replacement. While that relaxed me for a moment, she added I probably wouldn't need a knee replacement for another five years.

How did she even know that?

Once again, I was being told I'd need even more surgery down the road. Did everyone's body fall apart like mine or was I just *special*? Or had I simply been too hard on my body over the years, like friends had suggested? Clearly, something was up because my shoulder pain and back pain soon returned.

Around friends and family, I continued to put on a good front to show them I was OK. And that had always been very hard for me, faking it. At least I didn't have to fake it when I was by myself. In those isolated moments I could just be miserable. Later, I realized that letting myself fully experience the pain while alone was powerful, in a dark way. I was unencumbered by the need to pretend everything was fine.

Even after talking to Carl, I'd convinced myself that no one really wanted to hear about my pain. I continued my PT with Julie, now focusing on rehabilitating my new prosthetic hip. I always left our sessions feeling some improvement in my hip and shoulder. But the relief was short-lived, gone by the end of the fifteen-minute car ride back home. I began to develop a defeatist attitude. The hope I felt with Julie was always drained from me by the time I opened the front door at home.

Just before my two-week post-op appointment, I developed a burning sensation on the side of my right knee—so hot it felt like I could fry an egg on it. Concerned, Becky called the surgeon's office to let them know. Since we had a follow-up in a couple weeks, they told her my issues would be addressed in the next appointment. They didn't seem terribly alarmed, as I was still healing from surgery.

During the follow-up appointment, the physician's assistant (PA) assured me this burning sensation was all very normal.

I should've known. Normal pain. Live with it.

He explained that my iliotibial (IT) band, which is a long piece of connective tissue that runs along the outside of your leg from the hip to the shinbone, had been stretched during surgery and that was the cause of the burning feeling. He then drew a bell curve on a piece of paper to demonstrate the typical healing process. Pointing to the middle of the curve, he said, "This is where you are. Some people are better and some are worse."

I guess this was supposed to make me feel better, but it didn't. I wondered why the hell was he drawing a bell curve while I was sitting there in pain.

Intellectually, the explanation of the stretched IT band made sense, but something about the burning sensation on the side of my knee felt very wrong. Things should improve after surgery, not get worse, right? Over the next few weeks, I tried to convince myself the PA's explanation was accurate, even though it seemed like a lot of BS. The burning sensation was so intense, I had a hard time believing it was normal.

My next appointment was the one-month post-op checkup with the surgeon who performed the hip replacement. Knowing that he was a hip specialist, I decided to refrain from sharing all my other pains with him.

When I walked into his office, he watched my gait and proclaimed, "You're doing great."

Maybe he was right, but I sure didn't feel great. It almost sounded like a canned pitch. I told him about the burning sensation on the side of my knee, and he agreed with his PA: this was normal.

I then told him that during PT, Julie had me on the squat machine without weights, and while I had no issue doing that exercise, that night the burning sensation worsened.

His face became tense. "She should *not* be working on that type of lifting exercise with you at this stage of recovery. She should be working on flexibility and range of motion . . . and that's it."

I was surprised, as I had been working with Julie for more than three months and had gotten to know her well. She was very well respected among her peers, and she would *never* go against protocol. In fact, at every appointment she referenced a specific therapy practice. Was he trying to blame Julie for the burning sensation? This seemed like an attempt to avoid responsibility and take charge of the situation.

"Perhaps you have another structural issue going on," he said.

I looked back at him, biting my tongue and trying to understand what he was implying.

"Sometimes you can clear up one issue with a *successful* surgery and once that pain is gone another one can appear from a different structural issue, such as your spine. So, the whole time the pain along your spine was being masked by the first structural issue, your hip."

Man, I did not like the sound of that.

Perhaps sensing my upset, he shifted gears quickly and, when the checkup was done, with a big smile he said, "You're doing great and the hip looks great."

I thought my jaw was going to drop as he shook my hand. The appointment ended. I felt like he'd pulled some sort of Jedi mind trick on me! I felt he was trying to separate the hip, his responsibility, from everything else. My head was spinning, and my anxiety levels were spiking as I left his office. And though I still had the burning sensation on the side of my knee, painful glutes, and a sore back, I was confident that my new prosthetic hip was doing fine. And so was my surgeon, apparently.

The highlight of that summer was supposed to be the full solar eclipse, with the Tetons of Wyoming in the path of totality. Mikey would meet me and Becky for the event. Unfortunately, Jaimie and Kaylee wouldn't be able to go. Now, I'm no astronomer and have zero knowledge of the sky, but I was pretty excited for the whole thing.

A total solar eclipse occurs only when the sun, moon, and Earth are aligned in a straight line. When that happens, the sun is completely obscured from view. The path of totality is sixty-seven miles wide. Outside this narrow band, the sun will not be completely blocked. Our place in Wyoming sat smack dab in the middle of this path. Totality would last two minutes and twenty seconds at approximately 11:35 a.m.

A partial eclipse would last about an hour and a half before and after totality. The buildup to the eclipse was a great diversion for me. It gave me a chance to spend more time poring over maps to determine the best spot from which to view the eclipse. We decided to hike to the top of Horseshoe Bowl on the southern end of the Teton Range, which rises to about 10,000 feet.

We'd planned to make a day of it, so Becky, Mikey, and I started hiking with head lamps at 6:00 a.m. It was a cool morning, but the skies were clear, stars were out, and we knew the temperature would warm up once the sun rose. It looked like it was going to be a perfect day!

I'd had competing emotions that morning. On the one hand, I was excited for this adventure, but on the other hand I was concerned about how my glutes and back would respond to a hike like this while carrying a backpack. But as we continued up the trail and passed an alpine lake, I began to feel a little bit lighter, liberated—I definitely had more freedom flowing through me than I'd had in almost eight months.

Seeing few other hikers, we reached the top of Horseshoe Bowl around 8:30 a.m. We then traversed the high alpine ridge to the south, stopping at an outcropping that provided a clear view to the east, down into the massive Horseshoe Bowl and Jackson valley far below, where we would spend the day.

At 10:16 a.m., the eclipse started. For the next hour and eighteen minutes, as the sun was slowly being blocked by the moon, the temperature started to cool down. Because we were on a ridge, we had uninterrupted views to the east and west. To the west was Idaho and the Teton Valley with the Big Hole Mountains in the distance. To the east was Jackson Hole, backed up by the Gros Ventre mountains. There were two large raptors flying high above us and a handful of small birds playing and singing just below our position. Totality would happen sooner to the west. As the sun and moon began their journey to perfect alignment, we each secured our protective glasses, which were needed until the moment of totality.

The excitement grew among the three of us with every passing moment as the sky slowly darkened and the shadows sharpened.

With over ninety percent of the sun now covered, we heard a handful of people cheering from the west. As we turned in that direction, we saw the dark shadow cone fast approaching and suddenly engulfing us in darkness. The speed at which it happened was astounding. It became eerily quiet, cold, and dark. We grabbed our down jackets, removed our protective glasses, popped the champagne, and took it all in.

The corona, the ring of fire, was an incredible sight. Its light was well beyond anything anyone could create. While we were unable to see the sun at this point, I was struck by the incredible distance the light traveled from behind the moon.

This was not only a visual experience; I felt it in my entire body. The birds fell silent, and the raptors were gone. The wind that was blowing out of the west appeared to have changed, and its direction was now gently out of the east. All my senses were working that day, experiencing one of nature's powerful cycles—from light to darkness and back to light. Our hike down was equally special, as we ran into other groups along the way, sharing our personal experiences before continuing. My fears and anxieties took a back seat that day, as did most of my physical pains.

The next day, Mikey headed back to Bozeman and Becky was leaving for New Hampshire to get Jaimie ready for her freshman year of high school. I would stay two more days on my own. I dropped Becky at the airport for her 7:00 a.m. flight home. From there I continued further into Grand Teton National Park.

I'd planned to hike to Trapper Lake with my float tube and fly rod. Feeling great from yesterday's big hike, I was excited for this day's adventure. There would be no elevation gain; I would essentially be walking along the valley floor to a small, remote lake that sits right up against the base of Mount Moran and the Teton Range. About an hour into my walk, a sharp pain shot through my glutes and lower back. The area of discomfort seemed to grow with each step I took—as did my bitterness. What had started with so much promise quickly turned into disappointment. Why did my body respond this way to a relatively easy hike after I felt fine trekking to an elevation of 10,000 feet yesterday?

I knew what I had to do. I gently headed back to my condo and rescheduled my flight home. Depressed and confused, I headed back to New Hampshire early.

There appeared to be no consistency in my pain, and it was becoming increasingly frustrating.

As much as I wished it could be, I knew viewing epic solar eclipses wasn't the permanent solution to my problem.

CHAPTER 5

Spinal Fusion

Back in New Hampshire, Jaimie was in school all day and Kaylee was in Colorado for her sophomore year in college. That meant I no longer had to put a smile on my face for the girls. I wholeheartedly dove into using this extra time to hone my skills of isolation. It just seemed to be the path of least resistance.

When the weather and my body allowed, I would try to hike in the White Mountains in New Hampshire. Some days I would feel relatively good, while other days my body was riddled with pain. Whenever that would happen, Becky and friends would say I was probably doing too much. I certainly did not have the answers by a long shot, but I knew what they were saying did not add up. There was nothing familiar to this pain. My gut told me this pain had little to do with "doing too much."

One morning, Becky encouraged me to take my stand-up paddleboard out. I headed to the water, feeling motivated, and saw there were no waves, and the ocean was still and glassy. Perfect paddling conditions. I could do this. Paddling is low impact, and I thought maybe this core exercise would be good for my back. After a couple miles of easy strokes, however, my back started to light up. *Dammit.* My heart sank along with my positivity. I saw my take-out spot and paddled the last few minutes. One more activity I couldn't do.

When I got home, Becky watched me sulk past her, shoulders drooping, not uttering a word.

"Hon, maybe you're trying to do too much again," she said with concern.

"How, exactly? Paddling a few miles is like walking to the mailbox for me. How could that be too much? I have a new hip. And there's not supposed to be anything else wrong with me!"

Becky's face fell, and I turned and stormed off. I now see, what I failed to see then, how difficult this journey was on Becky. How painful it must have been for her to be shut out by the person she loved most.

Alone again, I wondered if there really was something structurally wrong with my spine or other hip.

+ + +

By the end of September, my back was bothering me consistently. My anxiety and fear levels had ramped up as well. Maybe my surgeon was right and I had a real issue with my spine. I ultimately decided to see *another* orthopedic surgeon. I started to number the doctors I'd seen in my daily journal. Counting a few whose names I'd forgotten, this next doctor would be the eighth I'd seen in the last eight months, and most were orthopedists.

At the appointment with doctor #8, I was diagnosed with degenerative disc disease. I had no clue what this meant or how it would affect my life. I did not ask any questions. I was frozen and not sure I even wanted the answer. However, as he spoke, doctor #8 did not seem terribly concerned and thought PT would help. It felt like things continued to pile up and, while he was not sounding the alarm bell, I certainly was. Now I was being diagnosed with a disease of the spine, and it felt like I was left to my own devices to figure out what the true meaning of this condition was and what the long-term implications were. But the reality of the situation was, I had a filter that translated everything I heard; I was hearing everything with a heavy flavor of "danger, doom, and gloom." However, not once did he take the time to explain, as I have come to understand, that forty percent of people over forty had this condition.

Unable to relax and just let my body heal, four weeks after I was diagnosed with degenerative disc disease and following plenty of PT with Julie for my back (with no improvement), I started to wonder if the fourth doctor I'd seen, the one who replaced my hip, was correct that a bad hip could cause pain in other areas of my body. We were well outside the two-to-four-month time frame that he had suggested for the second hip replacement. In an odd way, I'd hoped that he was right. I wanted him to just get in there and fix it. I wanted all of this finished. Done. Over.

I privately shared with Julie my decision to go back to the hip specialist, because I believed that my left hip was causing the back pain. *Hoped* it was causing the pain. After all, I figured another hip replacement would be much better than degenerative spinal disease. I'd been through one hip surgery before; what was another? While Julie said it was a good idea, her eyes told a different story.

But I needed to find answers. Fast.

A week later, patiently waiting in the exam room, doctor #4 walked in with a fake smile plastered on his face. His body was tense as he cleared his throat and looked down at his chart. This wasn't starting out well.

"Doc, my back is—"

"Your hip replacement was successful, but your hip pain was masking another problem . . . a structural issue in your spine."

"I guess that could be possible, but a month after my surgery you said everything looked grea—"

"You need to see a spine specialist."

I wondered if he'd misunderstood me, that perhaps he thought I was blaming him for all the other pains in my body. But that was the furthest thing from the truth. I was just trying to find an explanation and get some relief.

"Do you want to look at my other hip?"

He sighed. "You have degenerative disc disease. Make an appointment with a spine specialist." And with that, he stood up. The visit was over. He didn't even take the time to examine my left hip. The one he'd told me I needed to replace.

I left another appointment without clear answers.

When I got home, Becky and I agreed that I needed to see a spine specialist, but someone who saw many more cases than the small group of orthopedists I'd been working with. We were able to coordinate with a large medical center and scheduled two back-to-back appointments. The first would be with the spinal surgeon, and the second would be with a hip specialist. That would be doctors #9 and #10. These two doctors would provide continuity in dialogue—something that had been sorely missing with my current providers.

Armed with a stack of images of my body and dozens of pages of notes from the eight doctors I'd seen the past ten months, we set off to meet with doctors #9 and #10. Doctor #9, the spinal surgeon, was patient and thorough. He and his two assistants spent over an hour with me, asking many questions about my symptoms. Where do you have pain? What makes it worse? What makes it better? How long have you had it? Did you have any pain like this years ago? Stand on one foot. Touch your toes. Have you lost any strength? Have you had a problem urinating? Reach behind your back.

On and on this went. The surgeon and his two assistants then shuffled over to view the MRI image. They seemed to look at the

MRI without speaking longer than I expected. For a moment, I thought this was good news—if there was a problem with my spine, wouldn't it be obvious? This had to be good news.

Then the silence was broken. "That looks a little bit suspicious," the surgeon said.

Fucccckkk.

They told me I had stenosis of the spine, called foraminal stenosis. I'd heard that term before but had no idea what it was. My breathing became shallow as I sat on the exam table. The doctor told me foraminal stenosis is the narrowing or tightening of the openings between the bones in your spine known as foramen. Nerves pass through the foramen out to the rest of your body. When the foramina (the plural form) close in, the nerve roots passing through them can be pinched, creating all sorts of pains and sensations.

I looked down and fought back the tears. *How can this be happening? When will it end? Who can I trust?* When I composed myself, the doctor said, "That is what is happening to you. Do you have any questions?"

Questions? I was still processing what he'd just said. I knew it, dammit, I just knew it. Even with all the PT, there had been no lasting improvement. Unlike the prior diagnoses of arthritic hip and degenerative disc disease, this new diagnosis felt much more serious to me. He was so formal with his diagnosis, and listening to him describe how the openings in my spine were shrinking was terrifying.

Finally coming to terms with what he'd said, I asked, "So what does this all mean?"

"You need to avoid putting your back in extension. So, no more arching the back. That will put more pressure on your spine and pinch the vertebrae, which will cause more restriction of the foramina, where the nerves exit, increasing the irritation."

I nodded, but thought about how arching the back was involved in everything I loved. Hiking, surfing, skiing.

So I finally asked the question I'd been itching to raise since he'd said "foraminal stenosis": "So can I still be active outdoors?"

He sat at the edge of the table and crossed his arms while staring at me. "Definitely don't do any hiking. While hiking up, you are in the opposite of extension and rounding your back, in flexion, and that's OK. But the problem is, hiking down puts you in extension, which is not good for your back. Same with skiing, coming down you are in flexion, but standing in ski boots in the lift line you are in extension. So, no skiing. I'd avoid backpacks, too. You don't want to add any extra weight to your spine."

I'm sure he could see the disappointment spreading across my face, so he added, "But you can play golf."

Great. I suck at the one thing I'm allowed to do.

I wanted to say something, but it was like my throat was closed. This was more than simply the end of certain activities for me. I was at a life-changing crossroads.

Becky realized I was speechless and took charge.

"What are our options?" she asked. "How do we treat this?"

The doctor nodded. "Physical therapy can help, as can an epidural injection. The epidural steroid injection is a precise image-guided shot. It helps with irritated nerves in the spine. If you respond well to the injection, it can eliminate the pain."

I jerked my head up. "Great!"

Becky narrowed her eyes. "Are there any side effects?"

"Nothing to concern yourself with. It's very safe to administer."

Becky looked at me. I nodded.

"OK, well, how long does it last?" she asked. "Will he have to come in for more shots in the future?"

The doctor smiled. "It could last up to a year, but the average is right around seven months. And once it wears off, you can continue to have further injections."

What the doctor failed to mention—and what I have since

learned through my own research—is that over time the injections can become less effective, and there are published medical studies about the negative impacts of the injections. I now understand he was treating me through the lens from which he was trained. But then, I blindly trusted him to my own detriment.

Having regained my voice, I asked, "How soon can we do this? Can we do it now?"

"We'll have to get one scheduled," he said. "I'll have my staff look into that for you."

While they were checking on getting me on the books for an injection, Becky and I packed up our stuff and headed down the hall to our next appointment with the hip specialist. They escorted us to another exam room. While we waited, I was feeling pretty good about everything. I had been given an explanation and a possible solution. One that would simply require a spinal injection every seven months or so. I could live with that.

The hip surgeon, doctor #10, walked in and quickly put up the X-rays of my hips on the light box. I noticed he had the before-and-after right hip replacement X-rays.

"Whoever did this right hip replacement did an excellent job. As you can see here—"

"I'm having a lot of pain in my right glute and knee."

"Your left hip wouldn't be causing that," he said, before performing a few quick physical manipulations of my left hip. "This doesn't look that bad. I'd give you ten years before you need the left replaced."

What? First, I was told one to two years until I needed it replaced, then two to four months. Now ten years? He could see I was confused.

"My job is to replace hips. Yours isn't that bad. And it's certainly not the cause of your current pain."

I pondered my next question. I knew what I wanted to ask, but I wasn't sure I wanted the answer. I took a deep breath. "OK . . . you have the X-ray before I had my hip replaced. Do you think I needed to replace it?"

The doctor looked me straight in the eyes and without hesitation said, "No, I don't think you needed the hip replaced."

I sat unmoving and stunned. After a few moments, Becky and I thanked him for his time and the appointment ended. We were whisked back to see if the other surgeon had been able to schedule the injection.

Surprisingly, they were able to schedule me that afternoon for a spinal injection. After the procedure, they gave me a pain diary to record the level of my pain for the next two weeks to determine effectiveness of the injection.

As the days progressed, I tried to hold tightly to the hope that the injection would work. I resumed my routine, which now included filling out my pain diary. This proved more difficult than I would have expected. It was hard for me to nail down the location and intensity of the pain. Except my right knee; that always had my attention. The burning sensation seemed to be returning with a vengeance, as did my anxiety.

Over the next week, it slowly became clear that the injection had not worked, even though, at times, I tried to convince myself it had.

It was a cold, rainy night on the seacoast of New Hampshire when I placed the call to the doctor. I began by telling the doctor that I didn't think the injection worked. My knee was burning, and my back and glutes could hurt on any given day.

"Mr. Murray, you told my staff the pain had subsided. The pain diary you faxed us indicated you've been improving."

"I honestly don't remember writing that, but still, the burning in my knee is—"

"Your knee is not related to your spine."

"So what do I do about the pain in my—?" My eyes started to well up with tears.

"Look, you have two options. First, just live with the pain. Second, once you can no longer deal with the pain, I can fuse your spine."

I almost dropped the phone. I didn't even know what a spinal fusion involved, but it couldn't be good.

"Just this morning, I did surgery on a patient who could no longer live with his pain, so I fused his spine." His comment felt like a threat to me. I now wonder if he was even aware of how his description scared and intimidated me.

Now crying and trying to catch my breath, I said, "Can you please speak with my wife?"

I muted the phone and called for Becky. With a face full of questions, she took the phone.

"I need to get some air," I said. "Talk to the doctor."

"It's forty degrees outside and pouring rain!"

"Please, just talk to him."

She nodded. Becky had become my designated ears and voice when I had neither.

Once outside, the temperature and rain had little effect on me. All I could think about were my two options—live with the pain or fuse my back. Fuse my back! What did fusing of the spine entail? As I continued on my walk, my mind began to race with additional concerns: forget outdoor activities, how would I be able to contribute to the family, and would I be able to fake happiness long term?

CHAPTER 6

More Injections

The next few weeks leading up to Thanksgiving were not good. I had little to no contact with my friends and resumed my routine of lying on the floor and stretching all day. I'd wake each morning wishing I could hit the fast-forward button to get to the bedtime hour.

I seldom had pain when in bed. However, I would often wake during the night with anxiety and fear, made worse by the darkness. It would not be uncommon for me to wake and yell out in fear, shaking my body in hopes of purging what I was experiencing. Becky would always roll over and try to comfort me. Sometimes it would help, but more often, my emotions were simply too great. I would then get out of bed and retreat to the spare bedroom alone where I would ultimately pass out from sheer exhaustion.

Typically, my Novembers were filled with great excitement—fall hiking, and cool days cycling in New England, while early winter storms started to roll into northwest Wyoming. For the past few years, I had been able to get out to Jackson for some early-season ski-touring off of Teton Pass. Not this year. In fact, I now realized my passion for planning adventures had essentially evaporated. That part of my life no longer existed. I now just lived to get through the day.

Mikey and Kaylee were home from college for Thanksgiving. I was still refusing to burden the kids with my issues, so I put on a happy face around them. It was hard but I did it and, while I was not myself, it certainly gave me a sense of relief.

After stuffing ourselves at Thanksgiving dinner, the three kids searched for a movie they all wanted to watch, I retreated upstairs where Becky was getting into her pajamas. I was upset and my neck was bothering me. It took Becky a few minutes to realize I was not doing well. *She must be becoming numb to this.*

"I'm struggling with the kids," I blurted out. "I feel like I'm not being true to them. Maybe I should explain, but I'm not sure if that's the right thing to do. I don't want to upset them."

Becky came over and touched my shoulder. "Our kids adore you, and they want to know what's going on with you."

With Becky's encouragement, we walked downstairs where the kids were sprawled out on the floor and couch. I sat down in my usual soft, upholstered chair. Kaylee sat lounging with her long legs hanging off our big leather chair to my right. Mikey was on the floor leaning against that same big chair, and Jaimie, still a young teenager, was behind me in her normal position, standing in front of the mirror that hung from our wall. Becky stood in the background, leaning against the wall. Everyone was present.

I took a deep breath, already choked up, and let the words pour out: "Kids, I need to talk to you about something."

Because my voice cracked, they knew something was up. The room became eerily quiet.

I continued, with tears slowly beading down my cheeks: "I'm not doing well. I'm really struggling. My pains are just not going away, and I am having a hard time dealing with it all."

Fully crying at this point, I told them, "I love you guys so much, and it makes me very sad and very scared not to be able to do things with you like we used to. I don't know what the future holds for me."

I couldn't look at them. I held my head in my hands and continued, "Mom and I are doing everything possible to try to get me healthy, but I feel so bad that I'm not there for you like I want to be."

I lifted my head up and looked at each of them. Kaylee, eighteen at the time, had tears in her eyes and came over and gave me a hug.

Mikey said, "Dad, you'll get through this."

Jaimie and Becky didn't know what to say, since I had never so openly shared this with all of them. Sharing feelings had never been something I had ever considered. I was the strong dad. How would expressing my weaknesses help anyone? I now see the value and importance of talking about my emotions, and how, if I'd done so, I could have avoided so much suffering. Becky and Jaimie ultimately filled the space with their silent support.

This is what home is meant to be.

+ + +

After Mikey and Kaylee went back to school, I continued to search for answers, with more doctor appointments. They were so confusing. With my new diagnosis of spinal stenosis, we returned to one of the doctors I had seen months earlier, doctor #5. While she read the notes from the spine surgeon, she openly challenged his assertion of the stenosis being "severe."

"I am not sure about that," she said. "Perhaps it is moderate."

That was good news, but the good news did not last long. She had been encouraging me to get a stem cell procedure of the spine with a doctor she would recommend. And when I asked her, as our appointment was wrapping up, if the burning sensation in my knee would get worse, she said, "Yes, unless you get the stem cell procedure."

I immediately decided a cutting-edge procedure was the only way to fix all my problems.

Come December, I thought about how I had been living with pain for almost a year and felt as if I had lost my spirit. I could not imagine a day when I would have it back. While I never had considered suicide, I often thought about others who found themselves at the edge of darkness. And though I was not there, I was aware I was not far from it and hoped I would not reach that point.

I've heard so many people say that suicide is the ultimate selfish act. I now see it differently and recognize, based on what I was experiencing, how overwhelming the mental pain must be and that the only way to stop it is by turning out the lights. It's often an act of desperation to escape incredible mental pain. I was thankful when I realized I was not there. But I could relate.

Worrying seemed like a choice in the beginning but, ultimately, became something I could not control. I just could not escape that pattern of thinking and the perception that my body was failing me on a large scale.

Each doctor appointment had its own unique takeaways. I went to Boston to see another spine surgeon, doctor #11.

"I've been really anxious the past year," I said to him, "and am afraid that I will be disabled long term."

He looked at me and said, "You're being a little dramatic."

Maybe I was. Nothing was adding up. I had no indication that my pain would heal. That's why I was continuously searching for *the answer*. The litany of doctors wasn't giving it to me.

As we packed for our Christmas vacation in Wyoming, I wasn't sure how the two weeks would play out. Would I be able to ski? Should I ski? I was now entering the land of the unknown. We arrived in Jackson on December 20. And though I had opened up over Thanksgiving to Mikey, Kaylee, and Jaimie about my physical and emotional struggles, it was not something we ever discussed after that. Sharing with them that evening was a big step for me, but it would take a couple more years for that to become common. Now, however, I'm a champion for my kids as they discover and lean into their emotional world. Becky and I encourage all the kids to share and experience what they are feeling . . . both good and bad.

The next morning was cold. As I looked out the window, I noticed the dark blue sky and calm winds. The bright sun had created a sparkle on the white snow. It was stunning outside. We decided to ski a few hours at the resort. Even though I felt like a porcelain doll, fragile, it felt so good to be gliding on the snow with everyone. While I still had some aches and pains, nothing got worse after three hours of skiing. That evening, I played it cool with Becky. Afraid to get my hopes up, I downplayed the success I had on the slopes.

The following day brought more blue skies that would give way to a nice cold storm that started to roll in midday. The storm was forecasted to last about forty-eight hours. The next two days we spent skiing some light powder at the resort. As the storm was winding down, Mikey, Kaylee, and I decided to do a backcountry tour off Teton Pass the next day.

It had been cold for a few days with heavy snow, and we were confident we would find some deep turns. As we geared up the next morning, Becky lectured everyone about being safe in the backcountry and told Kaylee and Mikey not to let me lead and break trail in the deep, heavy snow. I always liked to take my turn breaking trail, but I thought it was probably a good idea that I let Mikey and Kaylee do the heavy lifting this time. It was exciting for me to be back in the red van driving up Teton Pass in a snowstorm. And instead of the storm winding down as forecasted, it appeared to pick up in intensity for the remainder of the day. Our visibility in the backcountry was down to feet, as the storm continued to wrap in heavy bands of moisture.

We could not have scripted a better day. It was truly a gift from above! When we reached the top of the peak, and after Mikey dug a snow pit to determine the snow's stability, we shuffled across the flat section of the mountain before we began our descent. With our visibility extremely limited, and since I was the one who knew the route, I went first. I knew there was a bank of trees at the end of the first steep pitch that would be our rallying point and safe place to stop. However, before I had a chance to push off, the snow gave way from under me, and I was quickly swept off my feet. I immediately knew what was happening.

Avalanche! My training took over as did my survival instincts. I let go of my ski poles and started swimming with my arms like I was doing the backstroke to stay above the snow and not get sucked under and buried. As I looked down the slope, I could see the bank of trees fast approaching as the speed of the avalanche I was in increased. I kept telling myself to keep my feet downslope, so they would impact the trees and not my head. I then thought about Mikey and Kaylee. *My kids!* I started screaming, "AVALANCHE, AVALANCHE, AVALANCHE!"

As I continued to frantically swim backward, I looked to my right and noticed Mikey standing tall. To my left, Kaylee also loomed over me, in that same position. I finally realized that not only were they not caught up in the avalanche, but there was also no avalanche. My mind had created this incredible illusion. It seemed like an eternity that I was in this avalanche, but it only lasted about twenty seconds. My mind had created a reality that was completely separated from the truth.

I gathered myself and got to my feet, and Mikey and Kaylee began laughing.

"Dad! Did you really think you were in an avalanche?" Kaylee asked.

I could feel myself blushing and laughed it off.

We then proceeded to finally push off for our first run, but before we did, while still standing on the flat section of the mountain, I said to Mikey and Kaylee, "Oh shit. It's happening again." The world I lived in lost its stability and structure. Everything around me began to swirl and appeared to suddenly move toward me like I was in a speeding jet. And I then lost focus. Though I knew I was not in an avalanche this time, I quickly dropped to the ground to try to gain some sense of control and safety.

It was a profound experience. The symbolism was not lost on me: everything coming crashing down on me without being able to do anything about it, just like the doctors who were telling me to do this or that, making me feel helpless and out of control. It was my own emotional avalanche.

That day I experienced the sheer power of my mind and how it can misinterpret danger. The combination of limited visibility, which I realized later had caused me to have an attack of vertigo, plus my already-full emotional bucket, had allowed my taxed brain to create a distorted reality of an imaginary avalanche.

For the rest of the day, I had an amazing time skiing in the Wyoming backcountry with two of my favorite ski partners, although I was shaken up by what my body was experiencing. Though I was not in pain, I was getting fatigued and tried to determine if it was from climbing all day in deep snow, or if it was a result of my degenerative disc disease, stenosis of the spine, or maybe my left hip. I had tremendous guilt hiking out that afternoon, subjecting my body to such strenuous activity while in chronic pain. However, I now realize physical activity was good for me and it was the anxiety that needed to be tamed.

The hike out to the road at the end of the day proved to be long and difficult because of the untracked, deep snow. Mikey and Kaylee struggled too. I found myself thinking about the position of my back as I was trying to get it out of extension and into a more neutral position.

The next day was Christmas Eve and with that came a return of the burning on the side of my knee. I was not surprised. I'd almost expected it because of yesterday's tough hike out of the backcountry. After four days of skiing and hiking in the backcountry without any pain, I was incredibly disappointed when the searing pain returned. I viewed this as a confirmation that the stenosis was the cause of this pain. Hiking while in extension. I was learning a whole new vocabulary of things to worry about. I was sure skiing was the cause, which was hard for me to accept.

Christmas Eve and Christmas Day were difficult, as I tried to hide my pain and disappointment from Becky and the kids. In addition to the return of my burning knee, my neck became very sore. All pain had become threatening to me, but it was the nerve pain, the burning sensation, that terrified me. It seemed to indicate a very serious condition.

While I'd been in Wyoming, even though I was not able to completely forget about my health problems, the pain and anxiety did not seem as all-encompassing. But that changed in startling fashion as soon as I got back on the East Coast. The anxiety, fear, and pain immediately returned during the hour-long car ride from the airport in Boston back to our home in New Hampshire. This would be a trend I would be unable to recognize for quite some time, but it would surface like clockwork. Wyoming was an escape for me. I was truly blessed to be so fortunate. I not only had an amazing family, but also had access to all the Cowboy State had to offer: world-class backcountry skiing, fly-fishing, and beauty that never stopped. When I would return home to New Hampshire, my body must have sensed the vacation was over, and pain, fear, worries would flood back. Logically, there was no reason for that to happen based on my good fortunes, but it did.

Up to this point, I had seen eleven different doctors, and I was absolutely convinced my healing would come from one of the invasive procedures they'd suggested. It's what I'd always understood:

Doctors would heal you via surgery or medication. Doctors who weren't listening. My unerring belief in specialists would be my downfall at the time.

Early in 2018, I met with two different doctors (#12 and #13) who could perform stem cell injections of the spine to alleviate my knee pain. I had been told these injections were the future of medicine, akin to the fountain of youth. I was told to just get on the train. One of these doctors even told me the stem cell injections would help with my back. On face value that sounded great, but I was not there for my back. I wanted help with my knee. When I asked again about my knee, he told me the stem cells would help, providing the stenosis was causing it. Was he saying that stenosis might not be the cause?

I felt like I was living in a pinball machine, getting bounced off the bumpers in a never-ending fashion. But make no mistake, I was a willing participant, always reaching in my pocket for another quarter to keep this game alive.

I realize now that my obsession with finding the source of my troubles often had more to do with my own emotional struggles than it did with any physical pain. The physical pain would turn out to be a symptom rather than the cause.

What was shocking was, at the time, I did not pay attention to my ability to be active and relatively pain free when I was in Wyoming. The dozen-plus doctors had convinced me that I had real structural problems with my body. So, I should be in pain no matter where I was, but that wasn't the case. Somehow in the mountains—my favorite place—whether during an eclipse or skiing with my family—my pain would often disappear.

How was I not able to recognize then the times I was pain-free? One of those enjoyable moments was when I was hiking with Mikey in the backcountry of southwestern Montana on a cold February morning. As we started to climb, Mikey was off like a jackrabbit.

He'd become an exceptional climber, effectively being able to manage the pain of skinning in deep snow. While I struggled to catch my breath and keep up, I took pride in watching him move with strength and agility up the mountain. The temperature was in the teens, and the sky had cleared and turned completely blue.

As we skinned up the mountain, we became excited with the great view of our ski objective and the rugged terrain. No one had been back in this area, so we needed to break trail. Mikey, being the kind of son he is, took the honor. We would ski three or four runs in the area. So, once the skin track was established, we would use that for the remainder of the day to access our ski lines. Our first few runs were fantastic—the snow, while not deep, was light and soft underfoot. I was feeling good, and we were having a great time together. Our conversations kept my mind off fuzzy, tingling sensations in my limbs that I'd experienced early that morning.

We had been eyeing one ski line all day, and it was much steeper than the lines we had been skiing so far. The starting zone was a small open bowl that was around thirty-five degrees. It then funneled into a choke, probably fifteen feet wide, only to open into a tree-free meadow that was not quite as steep for the remainder of the run. The whole left side was flanked by a cliff face that rose forty feet, with the right side lined with tall pine trees caked with our favorite wintertime snow.

We got to the top of the bowl and discussed how we wanted to ski it. We talked about where we would enter, what our safe zone would be in the event of a slide, and how we'd go one skier at a time and always have eyes on each other. Mikey took the lead in snow assessment and suggested that he ski cut the very top.

A ski cut is a stability test where a skier crosses an avalanche starting zone to see if he can initiate an avalanche. The idea is that if he does, he will be above it and ideally moving across to a designated safe zone. Mikey got in position with confidence, but he was certainly not cavalier about it.

As I patiently waited in my safe position, he cut across the very top of the bowl and, moving across, jumped up and down trying to put more weight on the snowpack. He got across, nothing released, so he gave me the nod, as he side-stepped his way back up to my position, ten or fifteen yards away. I offered him the first turns, and he accepted. He flashed the line, not quite straight-lining it, but there were no obvious turns either.

A fast skier, Mikey disappeared for a brief moment as he went through the choke area, only to reappear in the meadow below at a higher speed. His bright orange ski pants made for a great contrast and visual with the white snow and dark blue sky. He let out a scream of enjoyment as he stopped in our safe zone in a bank of trees at the bottom. I buckled my boots, adjusted my goggles, and yelled, "Dropping!" My pains and anxiety were distant memories. I was in the snow and in the moment.

Back at the van, we inhaled a few slices of pizza, downed some cold beer, and reminisced about the day's adventure. Mikey and I have a strong connection, and it was only enhanced by the endorphins that flowed through my body that day. In that moment, I considered staying in Montana for the evening, but I was committed to making the four-hour drive back to Jackson to ski the next day. I didn't want to miss what should be an excellent day in the backcountry skiing more powder.

I didn't recognize it at the time, but those adventures and planning those excursions were ways for me to dodge my fear and pain. I now understand that the mountains provided me with a great sense of relief that I otherwise would have been unable to experience. They were my escape from reality. The mountains and my son healed my pain.

CHAPTER 7

Twisted Pelvis

For all I had put Becky through the past year, as a Christmas gift I decided to treat us both to a week at Canyon Ranch, a wellness spa in Arizona. Though I was not into yoga or meditation at the time, Becky had become a dedicated practitioner over the past few years, particularly with yoga. I also thought this setting might allow me to let go of my insecurities about giving yoga a try—something Becky had been encouraging me to do for some time. She already knew it was a healing practice—though at the time she did not truly recognize the depth of that modality.

The more I studied the brochure I gave Becky, the more excited I became about the whole trip. In addition to offering yoga and meditation throughout the day, the spa also offered various one-on-one meetings with doctors, nutritionists, and a variety of therapists. The week I'd picked to go, Becky had a prior commitment the first night, so I went before her, not wanting to miss out on any of the stay. This healing trip was as much for me as it was for her.

As the week progressed, I was really starting to enjoy myself at

Canyon Ranch and took advantage of anything that made sense to me. It was a chance for me to find more answers. I signed up for a consultation called musculoskeletal and joint assessment. I would receive a full musculoskeletal evaluation to identify areas of impaired movement, mobility, or pain.

Perfect. That could really help me.

During the session, the therapist introduced herself as Margret and asked me to tell her a bit about myself. I quickly rattled off a slightly watered-down version of the last fifteen months of pain.

She was not a doctor. However, having read her bio, I noticed she seemed to have many credentials. Margret listened intently and seemed to be taking in what I was telling her. Yes, she listened. This was foreign to me after so long dealing with mostly dismissive doctors. She also seemed focused on how my body moved as one unit. She explained that she believed that my body was not moving correctly. And while she had not seen any of my X-rays, she told me, "I don't think the stenosis is causing the burning sensation on the side of your knee."

A wave of optimism washed over me. It was hard for me to completely grasp her detailed account of what was happening in my body, as my mind stayed anchored to her comments about the stenosis. But I held on to her positive prognosis like a precious gift. It was exactly what I wanted to hear!

She gave me a handful of exercises that she said would help with the alignment and movement of my body. I left excited and as if the weight of the world had just been removed from my chest.

I had the fear of God put in me by a number of doctors about my stenosis. "It can never improve," had been the constant theme. I was relieved now to have someone see something else. Since the burning sensation typically went away when I was active in the mountains, I left that appointment one hundred percent convinced she was correct with her diagnosis. And I could fix myself, according to her.

However, after a couple of weeks of doing the exercises she had suggested, nothing had changed in my body. In fact, I had never been so tight and restricted. I decided to send an email to Margret to see if she had any suggestions. She got back to me and encouraged me to pursue a provider at the Postural Restoration Institute (PRI).

She told me that PRI's concept is the body is not symmetrical. Respiratory, neurological, circulatory, visional, and muscular functions are not the same on the left side of the body as they are on the right. At the institute, they try to identify these imbalances and develop exercises to restore balance to the body. The exercises and stretches I had received from Canyon Ranch were based on this philosophy. I quickly located a local PRI provider and made an appointment with Tom Evans.

Toward the end of our first appointment, his conclusions were similar to Margret's. He also did not believe the stenosis was causing the on and off burning on the side of my knee. He said my movements were extremely dysfunctional, my breathing was very shallow, and I had a twisted pelvis. He said this was the cause of all the pain I had been experiencing the past year and a half.

He even pointed out that the arthritis in my hips was probably also from this imbalance that I have had my whole life. In addition to the twisted pelvis, I also had an anterior pelvic tilt, he told me, and added I would need to relearn how to move correctly. He seemed so confident in what he was telling me that in less than an hour, I was completely committed to him and to his approach. I had been looking for someone, or some positive diagnosis and treatment, that I could hitch my wagon to. I see how this behavior had me on an emotional roller-coaster ride. However, now I also realize there was a flip side to my unrelenting pursuit to heal—as it brought me closer to my ultimate solution. It was a journey I had to take. We spent the remainder of our first appointment walking, stopping only to make adjustments to my body to teach me a proper walking technique.

"Ribs down, arms swing naturally, head looking forward, rotate your pelvis and keep airflow moving deliberately . . . flow saunter," he said.

He told me that he was very confident he could restore balance for me. I was thrilled with the meeting and felt this was what might get me back to health. I was inspired as I drove home. Unable to contain myself, I called Becky to tell her how the meeting went. After about ten minutes of me explaining what we did and what he thought was the issue, I paused for a moment. Becky was quiet on the other end. Then I heard a sniffle.

"Are you crying, Beck?"

Crying louder now, she caught her breath and said, "I'm just so happy for you. You've worked so hard to find the solution, and now you might have it."

For the next week, I was constantly practicing the proper walking technique I had learned. I struggled with keeping my pelvis forward, only able to do so by fully engaging my core, which took some effort. Tom told me it would take time, as my pelvis had been in the wrong position for many years. For the next few weeks, I started to see minor improvements, only to have the usual glute, lower back, and side-of-knee pain return.

Another dead end.

This had to end. It was time to set up an appointment with a physiatrist. I'd learned they specialized in the nonsurgical treatment and the diagnosis of the musculoskeletal and nervous system.

Becky and I went to the first appointment together. The physiatrist—at this point, I think we were at doctor #15—told me because I had so many issues going on, we were going to take it slow.

"We're going to peel back one layer at a time and eliminate issues as we go," the doctor said. "It may take some time to get to the root of your pain. But if you persevere, we will find it."

We talked about the sensations and pain I had been having in both of my knees. He did not think it was foraminal stenosis, because it would be highly unlikely to have both right and left nerves affected at the same time. I asked him about neuropathy because my older brother had wondered if that was my issue. He seemed pretty confident that was not the cause.

I'd done some research online and told the physiatrist I wanted to be tested for a nerve disorder. I needed answers and would try anything. The test required an electromyography (EMG), a procedure that measures muscle function or electrical activity in response to a nerve stimulation of the muscle. The EMG involves inserting a needle into the muscle and sending an electric current through it to see how the muscle reacts. It can help diagnose a nerve disorder. It's a long and painful test. And I was ready for it.

When the test was over, my physiatrist looked over the results and told me I had neuropathy and that I needed to see a specialist. He told me not to panic, which, of course, I started to do.

Noting my concern, he added, "It doesn't seem extreme."

"What does that mean?"

"Just slow it down and get to a neurologist."

Days later, I became even more concerned. It didn't help that the neurologist (I'd lost count, but I'm almost positive he was doctor #17) had little personality. Not that I was surprised. It was pretty much what I would have expected from someone who worked on nerves. Mr. All Business reviewed the EMG results in front of me and told me that he wasn't sure about the conclusion and diagnosis and furthermore, the long and painful test I had done was not complete. He asked me if I'd be willing to do another EMG.

I closed my eyes and sighed. "Fine."

As he prepared my skin for the various needle inserts in my legs and arms, there was little conversation. He made no attempt to help me relax with small talk. The silence was killing me, so I told him that I'd been extremely anxious the past year and wondered if that could have affected my nerves.

I had told over a dozen doctors about my anxiety, and most had replied something along the lines of "You're being dramatic" or "You just need to relax."

So, I was shocked when this neurologist said, "Yes. Anxiety can absolutely cause nerve pain."

There was no time for follow-up questions, as he proceeded to shock my muscles for the next thirty minutes. Finally, at the end of the test, he told me that I did not have neuropathy. He also said the nerves were firing appropriately and that stenosis was not causing the pain either.

I was going to lose my mind, whether nerves were the problem or not.

I was back to square one. No answers and no relief.

PART 2:

Discovering the Mind-Body Connection

CHAPTER 8

Opening the Book

I had been living with pain for over a year and a half, seen seventeen different medical doctors, had dozens of images taken of my body, and had received two spinal injections and a full hip replacement. Unfortunately, after all that, I was no better off. I felt as if I was suspended in time, running out of options. The only solutions I'd been offered were either some sort of invasive procedure, like fusing my spine, or more injections, but that was more like a bandage than a cure. Was there no middle ground?

In June of 2018, Kaylee was spending the summer in Wyoming working as an intern for the Jackson Hole Conservation Alliance. Having her in Jackson was a good excuse for me to get back out to Wyoming. She's always fun to be around. An exceptional athlete in high school, particularly in lacrosse, Kaylee excelled in everything she tried. She has a wonderful free spirit and sense of adventure. We share the love of road trips and live music. The first four days of my visit were great. I hiked each day with her and Mikey, who came from Bozeman to visit us. We were not bagging any high Teton peaks, but I was outside exercising in the wilderness, which always helped me find some relief from my anxiety and pain. Each time we set off on a new adventure, though, a part of me still worried that the anxiety and pain would return.

On the fifth day, some rainy weather rolled in. Mikey headed back to Bozeman, and I hung out at the condo while Kaylee worked. By midmorning, by myself, the pain in my legs and feet increased. I had just spent four days in a row hiking with essentially no issues. On the one day I took off to relax, the pain had returned. The sensation of cold electric currents was passing through me. The fear and anxiety followed.

I was unable to sleep that night. Though my feet were not bothering me at that point, I couldn't stop worrying. What if the neurologist was wrong? What if I did have neuropathy? What if it was the stenosis, and the spinal surgeon and physiatrist were right?

Wide awake, I decided to grab the book my friend Carl had given me the previous year on how to live with chronic pain. Initially, I'd decided not to read it. After all, my goal was not to *live* with chronic pain, but to beat it. To my way of thinking, by reading the book I was accepting the pain. I did not want to believe that I would be living with pain for the rest of my life.

To be honest, my true belief was not that someday I would get better and therefore have no need to learn how to live with chronic pain. It was actually quite the opposite; I was scared to the core of my soul that I would never heal. Recognizing this fate frightened me more than anything.

I'd seen no evidence to believe I would heal. And while I still didn't *want* to read the book and risk acknowledging my pain destiny, I had enough curiosity to turn the light on and take a peek. Worst case, I thought, perhaps it would put me to sleep.

I skipped the introduction and started right in with Chapter 1 of John Sarno's *Healing Back Pain*. One of the first sentences caught my attention: The idea that pain means injury or damage is deeply ingrained in the American consciousness.[2]

Interesting. Why were those some of the first thoughts he'd put on paper? It would take me months to truly understand the effect those words would have on me.

Sarno explained that Western medicine viewed the body as a complex machine and believed that any illness was brought on when something in that machine was broken. He thought the medical community had become overly reliant on imaging, test results, and the need of physical proof for anything to be valid.

I read on, wondering when he would get to the pages of practical tips that would help me. As usual, I was looking for the ultimate answer in the form of a quick fix. Show me some bullet points or a checklist that could simplify the nuances of living with pain.

I continued to read. He wrote that physicians "tend to make a sharp division between the things of the mind and the things of the body and only feel comfortable with the latter."[3]

Reading this brought to mind all the doctors I'd seen and their responses when I told them about how I was feeling. It felt invalidating for them not to acknowledge my comments about the stress and anxiety I'd been carrying with me. I had shared my anxiety level with all the doctors, not because I suspected that my anxiety was playing a role with my pain; that never really occurred to me. Without knowing it, at the time, I was hoping to be comforted. I was looking for someone, anyone, to put their hand on my shoulder and say, "It's going to be all right." Unfortunately, that never happened. Clearly, my experience mirrored exactly what Sarno was saying.

I paused for a moment, closed the book, and read the title

---

2   John E. Sarno, *Healing Back Pain: The Mind-Body Connection* (New York: Grand Central Life & Style, 2010), 1.

3   Sarno, *Healing Back Pain*, 3.

again. Nowhere on the cover did it mention managing chronic pain. What I had failed to notice was the subtitle of the book: *The Mind-Body Connection*. I had been carrying this book with me for almost a year.

Why did I think it was all about living with and managing pain forever? Looking back, I now know it was my own fragile emotional state over my condition that had clouded how I saw and experienced the world around me. At that moment it became abundantly clear that the book was not about managing chronic pain—it was about healing a pain syndrome I'd never heard of before, Tension Myositis Syndrome (TMS).

Ironically, the book I had grabbed to put me to sleep quickly became fascinating, so instead of dozing off, I made a cup of coffee, moved out to the couch, and continued reading. Sarno claimed that repressed emotions could cause physical pain. While part of me found the idea radical and appealing, a part of me wondered if I was just grasping for yet another solution as I'd done so many times before. Was this an excuse to avoid accepting that my body was failing me?

Regardless of the reason, I was drawn to Sarno's theory because of his description of TMS. He was describing my pain. I recalled the neurologist in Boston who'd told me that anxiety can absolutely cause nerve pain. His remark connected to what Sarno was explaining in his book. As I continued to read, on each page something jumped out at me that I could relate to. I felt as if the book had been written about me, for my own healing.

Vocabulary I had become familiar with was showing up on the pages that I was quickly absorbing and turning. However, for once, the words didn't scare me, but rather helped to demonstrate the scope of the syndrome: degenerative disc disease, butt pain, anxiety, spinal stenosis, frozen feet, nerve pain, structural issues, arthritis, neck pain, shoulder pain, carpal tunnel syndrome, and heartburn. So many things I had experienced!

Sarno went on to explain the importance of *conditioning* as it relates to TMS pain. And how the subconscious brain can make an association with a certain activity, such as sitting, and sitting will then initiate the pain response. I'd essentially become programmed to feel pain.

When I'd first pulled my hamstring, it was always worse sitting down. I couldn't take my mind off it. Then the burning sensation on the side of my knee came. It was never a problem when I was skiing, but it was when I was sitting for Christmas mass. And then there had once been a traumatic frozen feet episode when I was sitting in my car, alone and scared. My symptoms began falling into place. Everything Sarno said described me to a T.

I was captivated by the book. As I read on, I learned that Sarno describes common patterns of pain and how it can become all-encompassing: "To some, the pain becomes the primary focus of their lives. They become obsessed."[4]

In hindsight, I see that my pain served two purposes. It was a distraction from emotional pain, but physical pain could also be viewed as a way my body was trying to get my attention: *Over here. Remember me? Can I get some service, please?*

According to Sarno, the physical pain is designed to create a distraction from those undesirable emotions. Sarno cites a number of case studies. Some had pain conditions similar to mine; others did not. But I could relate to all the stories, especially the hopelessness so many others had felt.

Many of Sarno's examples were of people in extreme pain. While I had times when my pain was significant, I was more affected by *constant* pain rather than the *degree* of that pain. Nonetheless, emotionally, I was being torn apart. And as a result, I was falling apart physically.

---

4   Sarno, *Healing Back Pain*, 30.

In the chapter "The Psychology of TMS," regarding the role of fear in TMS, Sarno wrote, "What things is the person afraid of or unable to do? Disability may be more important than pain, because it defines the individual's ability to function personally, profession-ally, socially, and athletically."[5]

I was moved by these words. Right or wrong, I had defined myself as someone who loved the outdoors and being extremely active. That's who I was. That's what I did. It's what I would talk about. I felt that my one true joy—enjoying outdoor activities—was being taken from me. And if that was taken from me, what would I do? What else was I capable of doing? I could relate to the emo-tions associated with the fear of having my life changed as a result of physical pain. But what I would come to learn is, how I chose to define myself controlled too much of my life. Changing how I viewed myself would require much unpacking on my part.

After reading many chapters, I suddenly felt a surge of positive energy run through me. I looked at the clock. Almost 11:00 p.m. That meant 1:00 a.m. back home in New Hampshire. Knowing Becky keeps the phone by her bed in case our kids need her, I sent her a quick text asking if she was awake. As I suspected, she replied pretty quickly. I told her to download *Healing Back Pain* by John Sarno ASAP. And I added, "I think I've finally figured out what's wrong with me!"

Becky asked which chapter she should read: "I might be able to read that chapter without buying the book," she texted.

I laughed. Becky, God bless her soul, often chooses the worst time to try to save money. I typed back in all caps: BUY THE WHOLE DAMN THING! LOL

Then, I remembered what time it was there. I told her to go back to sleep and we could chat the next morning. I continued to focus

---

5   Sarno, *Healing Back Pain*, 61.

on the book, consuming each page, ravenous for more information. By the wee hours of the morning, I'd finished the entire thing. It's ironic how the moment I accepted the reality of the situation—that I was experiencing chronic pain—I was able to open myself up to the possibility of a solution and a way out of my suffering.

Sarno's recommended treatment strategies:

1. Think psychological, not physical.
2. Abandon all physical therapy.
3. Resume all physical activity.[6]

Not wanting to lose any momentum with these concepts, I also took a picture on my iPhone of Dr. Sarno's suggested Daily Reminders. Some of those reminders included:

- The pain is due to TMS, not to a structural abnormality.
- TMS is a harmless condition, caused by my repressed emotions.
- TMS exists only to distract my attention from emotions.
- Since my back is basically normal, there is nothing to fear.
- I must resume all normal physical activity.
- I will shift my attention from the pain to emotional issues.
- I must think psychological at all times, not physical.[7]

I was all in. I needed to think psychologically. This would now be my course of treatment. I had seen so many doctors that past year and a half and still had pain. Now I wouldn't need to go to any

---

6   Sarno, *Healing Back Pain*, 91, 93, 96.
7   Sarno, *Healing Back Pain*, 97.

more appointments or search for explanations for my pain. I'd had my last image taken of my body. No more weekly massages. No more stretching obsessively. No more discussions about getting a platelet-rich plasma (PRP) or a stem cell injection in my spine.

In the light of Sarno's theory, I found my mental energy getting pulled in two directions. I had my new course of treatment to follow, but I also thought more about Western medicine and how it had failed me. While they perhaps meant well, the Western practitioners had unknowingly taken me down the wrong road, effectively creating more fear for me to carry along the way. I had bought into the concept that the *experts* knew what was best for my body. But what if they didn't? What if they were wrong?

Embracing my new treatment, I hiked with Kaylee each day. Before each outing, without disclosing to her my new course of treatment, I'd review Sarno's daily reminders. It didn't take long for me to have them memorized (part of my obsessive behavior) and they each flowed naturally—with the exception of one reminder: Since my back is basically normal, there is nothing to fear. What did *normal* mean? What did he mean by *basically*?

From a ten-thousand-foot view, I had TMS. There was no question in my mind. But as I became more granular in my thinking, things were not quite as clear. I tried desperately to put the doubts that were surfacing out of my mind and not overthink them. But, given my tendency to doubt myself, that proved to be difficult.

CHAPTER 9

Figuring It Out

A week after reading *Healing Back Pain*, I returned to New Hampshire, still excited about discovering Sarno's work. I spent many hours trying to determine what emotional baggage I had been carrying with me. If it was TMS, what was behind it? What was my mind trying to distract me from? While I recognized the stress and anxiety I'd been experiencing the past year and a half, I knew the emotional baggage behind the TMS had to be from something that had happened before the onset of my pain.

I thought about my days when I'd been working. There were certainly some emotional times back then, with many peaks and valleys. I had some insecurities and lacked confidence in certain areas of my work, but I'd thrived in others. I'd become so successful I was able to retire in my forties. In spite of the career challenges, I felt I'd dealt with those stressful times just fine.

I also thought about my education. I'd been a terrible student and had struggled from kindergarten right through college—I actually was held back in kindergarten—and was diagnosed with dyslexia around the age of nine. To this day, I'm still amazed I actually graduated from college and I have a recurring nightmare that I do not have enough credits to graduate from high school. Was this the baggage I was carrying?

I thought I had it all figured out. It was as simple as that, one, two, three. I understood it was psychological and not physical, as Sarno had suggested, and all the structural abnormalities were simply incidental findings. Now, I thought I'd discovered my repressed emotions—my insecurity about school—and I believed that realization would release me from the grip of chronic pain. My black-and-white mentality was emerging yet again. I was excited—but of course nothing is that easy. I had only scratched the surface.

As excited as I was, I was still on edge and not ready to socialize much. It seemed easier to be by myself, not having to share my struggles with others. We'd planned to spend the month of July in Wyoming with family and friends, which I was looking forward to, but as June wore on, my pain started to tick up in my feet and hands. My glutes and lower back were also incredibly tight. All of it was pretty low on the pain scale, but I always lived in fear. Would it be back? When? And then the worry kicked in: *What if it was not TMS? What if my self-diagnosis was wrong?* Back and forth I went. Worry about my diagnosis seemed uncontrollable. And telling myself *not* to worry seemed to only strengthen that urge.

As we got closer to July, I became increasingly anxious about the vacation. I was the unofficial tour guide, something I loved. But what if my body failed me when we were out there? What if I couldn't do the overnight backpacking trip we'd planned? What if my anxiety took over? Round and round I went.

Becky reminded me of how active I'd been each time in Wyoming.

And she assured me that even if I couldn't do it all, it would be OK. "We'll be with everyone we love," she said.

"Thanks, Beck. I suppose if it is TMS, the best thing to do is get out there and get active!" I smiled and felt as if a massive weight had been removed from my chest. I could breathe again!

Becky always knew the right thing to say. We'd met our senior year in high school and had started dating after a rousing New Year's Eve party a mutual friend threw. We instantly connected over our mutual love for outdoor adventures, sports, and mild competition on the tennis court or over a hand of rummy. After more than twenty-five years of marriage, she knows me like no one else and probably had a sense that I would rise to the occasion of our friends' visit.

It had been a couple of weeks since I'd learned about TMS, and I was still operating under Sarno's theory: It was my mind creating the pain. I had reread his book—three or four times—and yet, I felt no measurable improvement, other than a bit more optimism and confidence that I was on to something. Then one afternoon, I grabbed the computer to see if there was anything online about TMS. I quickly found a number of links to Sarno's books and his work. I continued my search and came across a blog for all things TMS. I spent the next hour reading posts. I couldn't believe it, there was an entire community for TMS. I was not alone!

I joined the forum, signed in, and made my first post. I described my symptoms: pain in my glutes, back, carpal tunnel, and heartburn. But what was really on my mind was the struggle I had with frozen feet. Was it TMS or neuropathy or stenosis? I was holding on to TMS, but that was a self-diagnosis after reading one book written twenty years earlier. That was a stretch, and I knew it.

I wanted to know if anyone else had frozen feet. Within a couple of hours, I had a reply.

It was from Warm Soaring Owl. Her response:

"My advice is to immediately drop the desire to compare yourself to others, to try to find your symptoms among others, or to describe any of your symptoms in detail."

Ouch . . . She's not warm, that's for sure. She had more to say, but I couldn't get past her comments and the need to correct me. Her words hit me and hit me hard. It was not what I wanted or expected to hear. I wasn't ready for that kind of advice yet.

I stewed over her comment for about ten minutes and then continued to search the website for other tools that might be helpful. I came across a list of doctors who treat TMS. There were less than a dozen names on the list and based on the timestamp, a lot of the information appeared to be dated. As I looked at the names, one caught my attention, Dr. Marc Sopher. Why did that name sound familiar?

Calling out to Becky on the back porch, I asked her if she'd ever heard of Dr. Sopher. She said, "Yeah, that was Mikey and Kaylee's doctor when they were young." Of course. Marc Sopher. I'd never met him, as I was working ten-hour days at that time, but I did remember his name now. I viewed this connection as a sign that I was on the right track. I wanted TMS to be my diagnosis; I wanted my body back and I embraced anything that would point me in that direction. I was far more threatened at the thought of the pain being caused by structural problems than by mental or emotional ones. Because as I would come to see, I placed too much value on my outdoor physical pursuits. I was always comfortable and at peace being outdoors and active, and the idea of that being robbed from me was unbearable.

I knew Marc was no longer practicing and had retired, but I convinced Becky to send him an email with my story. Two days later, he responded:

Hi Becky and Mike,

I am very sorry for what you've been experiencing, Mike, but pleased that you are interested in TMS. While I always tell people that I cannot make a diagnosis via email, I do think the history you offer is most likely to be consistent with TMS and similar to many I have helped.

In my experience, most of the persistent and chronic pain and other unpleasant symptoms we experience are due to TMS. Many are able to get better on their own, by reading and re-reading Dr. Sarno's and my books and staying focused on the approach. It is a matter of learning to think differently about how the mind may affect the body and create very real physical symptoms. The symptoms will leave once you fully understand and accept what is causing the symptoms. You must eliminate any doubt as to what is causing the symptoms (think psychological, rather than physical). This is a simple concept, but sometimes difficult to do when you have been conditioned to believe otherwise and are pursuing physical treatment for it.

Don't despair—you have the necessary knowledge to get better.

Sincerely,
Marc Sopher, MD

I now had my new marching orders. Read Sarno's *Healing Back Pain* again and order Marc's book *To Be or Not To Be . . . Pain-Free*.

While purchasing Sopher's book on Amazon, another book caught my eye: *Explain Pain* by David S. Butler and G. Lorimer Moseley. I ordered that as well. What I did not know at the time was that *Explain Pain* would have as much impact on me as Sarno's *Healing Back Pain*. As I waited for the books to arrive, I took the opportunity to reread Sarno's book.

While I fully embraced TMS based on Sarno's experience (which was clearly my experience), something was missing. I needed more.

Moseley and Butler used current research and science to explain pain. I was learning through reading *Explain Pain* that the brain is responsible for *all* pain. And that pain is a protective mechanism, and it's not always an indicator of tissue damage. Their book also explained the complexity of pain and how pain depends on the brain interpreting a massive amount of information sent to it through sensors. Pain is often from learned patterns of the nervous system. Using modern neuroscience, *Explain Pain* discussed how pain is a response to threats in our body, which are influenced by our thoughts. It also explained that as pain persists, the nervous system gets better at producing more pain.

They explained how these sensors work with the following example: "If you go to the dentist and have a shot, the chemical in the injected drug closes the sensors so they can't detect stimuli. This means that no impulses go to the spinal cord and onto the brain." In other words, no pain! They also stated, "Other drugs and chemicals can keep the sensors open. For example, the sting of a stingray, regarded by anyone who has been stung [by one] as the most painful thing they have experienced, works by locking [these] sensors open."[8]

Perhaps my mind had determined that physical pain was better than dealing with my repressed emotions. And now my physical pain was creating my anxiety, and the anxiety was creating more pain. In short, I was perpetuating a vicious cycle.

I arrived back in Wyoming the first of July ready for an extended visit to the Tetons. I was feeling very confident after reading *Explain Pain*. Everything made much more sense to me. All I needed to do was address all my repressed emotions. How hard could that be?

The first couple of days, I spent time fly-fishing on some of the local rivers and creeks. Besides stiff glutes and some lower back pain

---

8   David Butler and G. Lorimer Moseley, *Explain Pain* (Australia: NOI Group, 2015), 31.

in the late afternoons, I felt pretty good. Then, determined to take Sarno's advice to the fullest, I decided to go for a mountain bike ride.

There had been a five-year period when the kids were younger during which I did a lot of mountain biking, but I gave it up for road biking. Of course, after being diagnosed with degenerative disc disease and foraminal stenosis, I was advised to stay away from any type of pounding activities. So, I was sure my days riding tough, rugged singletrack were over. But now that I was committed to rejecting the conventional diagnosis, I gathered my mountain-biking gear and made my way to the top of Teton Pass, ready to follow the same route of my typical ski tour in the winter.

I'd never been there without snow, so I was excited about riding the open bowls and ridge lines with the wildflowers in full bloom. It was the first time I'd ever mountain biked in Wyoming. It was a beautiful day, and I enjoyed the hour-long climb to the top of Mount Elly. The scenery was quite spectacular. After I reached the summit, I dropped down the backside of Mount Elly via an almost endless number of switchbacks. It was a demanding ride, requiring complete focus with both hands constantly applying pressure to the brakes. Once I reached the bottom, I stopped and looked up to where I'd come from. I was used to seeing that same view covered in snow, and it was exciting to see it in a new season.

I took a sip of water and tried drying my sweat-drenched palms for better gripping power before heading down to the last section through Black Canyon. The canyon is a five-mile runout. With steep slopes on each side of me, I knew there would be little room for switchbacks, and the single track would be fast and furious. As I descended through the canyon, I could feel the air get warmer as I dropped in elevation. I also noticed my hands were becoming fatigued from having to keep pressure on the brakes to keep a safe speed.

Instead of pulling over to take a break and shake my hands out,

I looked for a spot on the trail where I could remove my hands from the brakes to rest them, but I needed to do it in a spot where I could handle the increase in speed. Once I found a place, I let go of my brakes, eager to give my hands a rest. I'd gotten distracted by the sound of the babbling brook to my right, which caused me to lose my concentration for a split second. When I refocused, I found myself barreling toward a sizable rock.

Normally, if I was paying attention and had my speed controlled by holding on to the brakes, it would have been easy to roll right over the rock. Instead, I tapped the front brake precisely at the wrong time and I lunged forward, tumbling over the front of the handle-bars. With the steepness of the trail in front of me, I knew I would drop about eight feet or so before I would slam onto the ground.

Landing hard on my back and neck, I felt my bike bounce off of me seconds later. I lay still on the ground, not sure if I was injured. I was scared. I was still four tough miles from the road and civilization. I had not seen anyone since I'd started the ride, and there was a good chance no one would find me. I got to my feet, shaken, and quickly took inventory. Starting with my neck, I gently rolled it back and forth. It seemed fine. I then did some forward bends to make sure my back was OK. It was. I then cautiously moved my new pros-thetic hip in a circular motion. No pain. I was damn lucky.

Twenty minutes after the accident, I retrieved my bike, which had dropped off the trail after the crash. Feeling much better, as I prepared to move on I noticed a bright red color on my neon yellow bike and realized it was blood—and lots of it. I dropped the bike and immediately looked at my legs. They were fine. I then looked at my arms and saw they were cut up pretty badly.

At that moment the pain from the lacerations took over. I didn't think I would need stitches. But I had wounds all over and they were suddenly painful. Both of my palms were bleeding. I noticed I had a small but deep cut on my thumb. My right forearm was bleeding, as were both elbows. It was a bad crash, so I was not surprised at the damage that had been done to my body. But I was surprised that it took almost twenty minutes for me to realize I was bleeding and, more important, to feel any pain.

I then thought about the book I'd just read, *Explain Pain*. My brain must have thought it was more important for me to focus on the possibility of serious injury than any pain. Once my mind had determined I was no longer in danger, I was then able to see the blood. And that's when my brain initiated the pain response. On my ride back to the condo, I wondered, if I hadn't seen the blood on my bike and arms, how long would it have taken me to feel any pain?

I'd just witnessed firsthand how the brain controls our pain signals and decides when we should or should not feel pain. It works both ways. The brain can send pain when there is no injury or damage to tissue, or the brain can repress pain when there is an injury. Regardless of why the brain initiates pain, that pain is very real.

✦   ✦   ✦

The rest of the month was amazing: thirty days straight of outdoor adventure. My only course of treatment was a morning ritual of reviewing Sarno's daily reminders (My pain is not from a structural abnormality but is caused by my repressed emotions. There is nothing to fear, and I must resume all physical activities.), as positive reinforcements that I was not broken. I also fly-fished, hiked, biked, white-water rafted, and took an overnight backpacking trip—sleeping high up in the Teton Range with Jaimie, Kaylee, Mikey, Becky, and our good friends Mia, Maddy, Christian, and Dan. All my pain had been reduced to light sensations. Though I was still very tight in the hips, glutes, and lower back, the pain never seemed to get worse or prevent me from doing anything. Sarno's recommendation for upping the action in my life was clearly working.

I always hoped that the reduction in pain while in Wyoming would carry over to my time in New Hampshire. Unfortunately, that seldom happened. It always felt like I'd take one step forward and then two steps back. I would later learn that healing was rarely a straight line and that, like life, there would be many unexpected twists and turns. I would also come to understand that this pattern was becoming well embedded in my neural pathways. This is exactly what Sarno was talking about when he spoke of *conditioning*.

I needed to uncondition myself. And fast.

CHAPTER 10

Mind-Body Diagnosis

Back in New Hampshire, it quickly became apparent I had not broken the pain cycle I was in. The sensations I had in my legs and arms would often cross the threshold and leave me in misery, and I became less active because of it. Or perhaps I had more pain because I had become less active. I couldn't tell. What I did know was, I felt stuck in the pain place. It was at that point I made the decision to seek out a trained TMS doctor to see in person. Although I'd received the email from Dr. Sopher saying that it sounded like TMS, I wanted, or more likely needed, to hear it directly from a practicing doctor.

After researching qualified mind-body doctors, I settled on Dr. John Stracks, who was in Chicago. Before the appointment, I spent time learning as much as I could about him. I was moved by how brave and open he was about his own personal struggles with TMS pain.

I flew out to Chicago in mid-August and would meet with Dr. Stracks the day after my arrival.

I was nervous walking into the doctor's office. The Chicago humidity only added to my discomfort. I spoke freely for over an hour, sharing my passion for the outdoors, the onset of my pain and how it had impacted me, and my many, *many* doctor visits and competing diagnoses. He listened intently and took notes the whole time.

I was thrilled. He *listened!*

After I finished giving him my history, he conducted a brief physical examination and reviewed the medical records I'd brought with me. We then sat in his office, and he told me that after he meets with patients it can often be difficult for him to make a diagnosis of TMS. He said that is because things are not always quite as clear and conclusive. But then he looked directly in my eyes and said, "This is TMS."

I thought I would have had a sense of celebration or relief with his confirmation that my pain was related to my mind as much as my body. But I felt nothing. While TMS resonated with me in a deep way, I still did not understand my underlying issues and the TMS path to potential health.

I had searched and grasped for an answer that made sense to me for over fifteen months. And now I believed I had it, even though I had not discovered any deep, repressed emotions, the way Sarno described those with TMS would. In fact, other than reading Sarno's book and *Explain Pain*, in the grand scheme of things, I had barely scratched the surface of emotional work. I was still in the dugout, waiting for my turn at the plate. I think I was confused with the meaning of "repressed emotions." I was looking for past experiences that I did not remember to suddenly appear. I'd missed the obvious meaning: that repressed emotions are emotions that you unconsciously avoid (perhaps consciously too). I did, however, have anxiety, physical pain that would randomly appear and move around, and a sense of hopelessness. And now on top of what I gleaned from Sarno's book, I had an educated physician confirming this diagnosis. And though I would question the TMS diagnosis in the months and years ahead, I always came home to it. After Stracks finished speaking, there was a pregnant pause and then, with a shudder in my voice, I asked, "Can I heal?"

With his nonthreatening, Midwestern demeanor, Stracks said, "Yes." He told me that I may need to take it easier on my body in the future. Immediately upon hearing that, my body became very tense. As he continued to talk about healing, he said there may be lingering sensations. Again, I was hit with a wave of fear and had a hard time accepting there might be even one remaining pain site. My stomach turned just thinking about those "lingering sensations." My reaction to his comments was startling at the time. It happened instantaneously. I would come to learn my pain-body was being *triggered*. And those triggers would leave me feeling completely raw and vulnerable.

I couldn't imagine *always* having some sort of pain or sensation. It was not clear to me at the time, but my emotional suffering was significant. And while I intellectually accepted Sarno's theory on repressed emotions causing pain, I had yet to grasp what that truly meant, the relationship between my body and my mind. As I would learn later in my journey, resistance to pain played a major role in maintaining pain.

Stracks suggested that I participate in his nine-week course for TMS healing, which would start about a month and a half later. I eagerly agreed. Walking back to the hotel, I still felt surprisingly emotionless. I'd been secretly hoping I'd feel as if I'd just won the lottery. But nothing really had changed and, down deep, I knew this was just the beginning of a long, emotional journey that would have many peaks and valleys. I didn't know then that I would have many moments where I would want to quit, only to realize quitting was not an option. I had been close to the abyss a number of times and stepping back into the darkness could have been a point of no return for me.

I called Becky and told her about my official TMS diagnosis, though I didn't share much with her about how I was feeling—or not feeling—at that moment.

Becky was thrilled. I could hear it in her voice. She was also happy that I was headed to Wyoming to spend time with Mikey. She knew how important and uplifting spending time with our kids is to me. And of course, with my TMS diagnosis, that kind of positive emotion and outdoor activity would mean less pain for me.

I planned to catch a flight to Wyoming where I would meet Mikey for a week of fly-fishing in and around some of Yellowstone National Park's finest backcountry waters: Bechler River, Lamar River, Soda Butte Creek, Pebble Creek, Fall River, and the Upper Snake River.

The next seven nights were spent camping in and around Yellowstone National Park with Mikey. We experienced some of the finest trout waters in the world. For our last adventure of the week, we would fish the upper meadow of Fall River, which lies in the southwest corner of the park with the water originating from the heights of the Pitchstone Plateau. There are no roads or trails that access that part of the river. It is wild and remote, and that's why we were there.

We started our two-mile bushwhacking from Ashton-Flagg Ranch Road to the river, using the GPS on our phones for navigation. If you are adventurous, Ashton-Flagg Road is a fly-fisherman's dream, with endless opportunities for those willing to hike, as well as for those seeking solitude. The road, passable only four months a year due to heavy snowfall, is a rugged fifty miles that connects Ashton, Idaho, to Flagg Ranch in Wyoming, which sits between Grand Teton National Park and Yellowstone National Park. The road was built in the early twentieth century to bring material from Idaho to build the Jackson Dam in Wyoming.

This is grizzly bear country, and I even read that they will relocate aggressive grizzlies to this area because of its remoteness. With bear spray at the ready, we were off through the open forest of the tall, skinny lodgepole pine trees. It was beautiful, even though the forest is partially burned out from the Yellowstone fires of 1988. After an hour and half of hiking, we broke out into the meadow section of Fall River. The river is about fifteen feet wide and twists and bends its way through the tall green grass for a couple of miles before it dives into a small canyon below. Excited to be there, we wasted no time and set up our fly rods and tied on the appropriate flies. Though there was a chance for trophy-size trout in these waters, the real prize was just being there—where we would see no one!

The water was cold, clear, and slow moving. It is very easy to spook the native cutthroat trout. You need light, thin fly-line, and the fly needs to be landed on the water softly and on target (not my specialty). Typically, on water like this you have one shot. After working a half dozen bends with no luck, I started to lose focus. As I cast my #16 green drake fly upstream one more time, it drifted with the current toward a fallen tree. Instead of staying focused on my fly on the water, my attention was pulled toward the sky. Too late, I saw a large dark shadow dart out from underneath the tree and take a hard run at my fly. It was one of the largest trout I had ever seen, only made bigger by this small river it called home. And I missed it.

Truth be told, because of my loss of focus, I never even had it. Like the effects of a shot of espresso, though, I was filled with adrenaline from that brief encounter. I turned to Mikey, who was not far from me, and said, "Holy shit, did you see the size of that?" He shook his head, not even listening to what I was saying, as he was deeply invested with the float of his fly (like I should have been with mine). I repeated the same cast but knew I'd missed the opportunity. Mr. Cutthroat had moved on.

Even though we were on the river all day, I ended up catching only a couple of small trout, always releasing them with care, back to where they belonged. But that did not take away from the joy we experienced that day. In fact, the whole trip was great, and besides being preoccupied at times, the only symptoms I had that week were some very tight glutes and lower back, but it was never too bad. Was it true, then, that lots of activity reduced the TMS pain? I didn't want to get too excited, but it certainly seemed that way.

I always resisted when anyone suggested any of my symptoms were age-related, even at fifty-two years old. It wasn't my ego talking either. It angered me to hear comments about my age because it made me feel misunderstood. All of my pains came from out of the blue, not during my normal physical activities. And surprisingly, most occurred when I was idle. I knew that was not how age-related pain manifested. Because I had no explanation for my pain, I became aggravated, but I just knew it had absolutely nothing to do with my age. I paid attention and tried to make sense of my body's stiffness. What was the relationship between TMS pain and physical activity? How would an area of my body experiencing TMS pain react when met with physical exertion? What if I had had an increase in TMS pain after hiking all day? I turned over these questions in my mind and tried to remember if any of my readings had addressed them.

I was home for two days when I received a follow-up email from Dr. Stracks. He said he was checking in to see how I was feeling, what I was currently doing for TMS recovery, and how my fishing trip to Wyoming went. He also said that since his TMS course did not begin for a few weeks, he could get me started on some homework before the first class.

His email made me feel newly inspired. I told him I'd continued to read up on TMS, exercised each day, had done some heavy outdoor activities on my trip. I was considering giving yoga another try, if I could just get the nerve, and reconnecting with family and friends. I mentioned I still had anxiety and fear when thinking about the pain, what it might mean, and what it could become. I said that if you could put me on a river casting a fly, the nerve pain in my legs all but disappeared. What I shared with him was more to assure myself that all my pain was attributed to TMS.

At ten o'clock that evening he wrote back:

Hi, Mike,

You've done so much already; you have done great work. Don't lose sight of that. Attached is a handout on "self talk" I really like, so this is your homework for the weekend.

It's definitely going to be on your mind, so don't fight it. It's a meditation puzzle—allow the worry to come into your mind, don't fight it, and allow it to flow back out. Even better if you can replace it with something positive.

So, read the handout, go to a yoga class over the weekend, and start to wonder if your body is expressing an emotion (fear, sadness, anger, etc.). We'll talk more about emotions in a few weeks but think about whether that may be part of what your body is expressing.

Check in with me Monday or Tuesday, and I'll give you another assignment for next week.

Dr. Stracks

His words and shared resources were so reassuring. This man cared about healing people. Most important, he *listened*. Stracks had shown more compassion in the short time I'd known him than all the previous doctors combined. It had become clear to me that most doctors, at least the ones I had met with, viewed emotions as playing no role in chronic pain.

When the mind-body class started toward the end of September, I had some tingling sensations in my arms and hands. They weren't painful, just heavy enough to hold my attention—a classic TMS case, as if right from Sarno's book. I still had tightness in my glutes and lower back, and fuzzy feelings from the knees down to my feet on both legs. The leg sensations often had crossed the line and become painful. The pain could take the form of frozen feet, burning on the side of my knee, or, occasionally, the feeling of severe shin splints. I never knew what would initiate the pain. Besides noticing the decrease in pain while in Wyoming, I was unable to recognize the difference or maybe the importance between light sensations and pain. It was all the same to me. I seemed to have lost the ability to know the difference between sensations and pain.

Six people, me and five others, took Stracks's live Zoom online course; three men and three women. The youngest was in her twenties and the oldest was eighty. Each of us was living with chronic pain to varying degrees. Dr. Stracks talked about recovery and said that, while Dr. Sarno claimed healing could occur by simply reading and rereading his book to understand that the mind creates the pain, Stracks's experience with patients was very different.

He found that few people healed in that fashion. He cautioned each of us that recovery was not a straight line and to be prepared: "You will have two steps forward, one back, three sideways, and two more forward." Looking back on this part of my journey, it's now clear that while I heard his comments on setting our expectations for healing, I failed to absorb them.

In the mind-body class we covered—

- Journaling
- Self-talk
- Meditation

- Self-kindness

- Emotions

- Boundaries

- Catastrophizing

One of the first things we talked about was journaling. Other than seeing Becky occasionally with a notebook, I had no idea what journaling meant and how it could help. Dr. Stracks handed out material that contained studies on the positive effects of journaling on your health. One of these studies was conducted by Dr. James Pennebaker, who says journaling allows for self-expression, which could reduce stress, improve your immune function, and strengthen emotional functions. Identifying and labeling your emotions and difficult moments in your life, according to Dr. Pennebaker's work, would have positive results. While I tried journaling during the workshop, I grew impatient because I wasn't feeling any of the benefits yet. Plus, it felt forced and awkward. In retrospect, I should have given it more time.

One of the prompts that Dr. Stracks gave us to journal on was gratitude. While I recognized that I truly had much to be grateful for—a wonderful wife, three healthy, contentious, smart kids, and long-term financial security—I couldn't understand how acknowledging my fortunes would translate to relief of pain. Trying to actively manifest or manufacture gratitude in words was difficult, and I grappled to put anything meaningful on paper. Then one afternoon, struggling to journal and feeling very down, I decided to jump on my road bike and go for a twenty-five-mile ride to see if I could shake the blues. Within fifteen minutes of being on my bike, my dark mood dramatically changed. I went from being down and somber to happy and alive. My mind naturally drifted to positive thoughts like family, fly-fishing, skiing, and even our two corgis,

Bernie and Sweet Lou. It was amazing how my feelings could change so quickly. Then I started to think about my experience journaling and the word *gratitude*. Family, fly-fishing, and skiing are all things I am grateful for. It was so simple and obvious now.

Still on my bike, my speed increased. I realized that fear and anxiety could not exist with gratitude. They can't occupy your mind at the same time. If you could be and feel grateful for something, fear and anxiety could not be present. It was a real aha moment for me.

I was on to something so I started journaling every day, writing five things I was grateful for, with the hope that focusing on gratitude would eliminate the fear and anxiety that plagued me. But what I also learned is, actual gratitude cannot be manufactured. Simply writing down things you are grateful for will not automatically bring you to the space of ease, freedom, and happiness. At least it didn't for me. Disappointed at first by this realization, I came to understand that it was me, again, looking for the quick fix. And in this situation, there simply wasn't an easy answer. There was no way around it, I was going to have to go through it.

Dr. Stracks proved to be a valuable resource. In addition to what we were covering in the mind-body class, he also introduced us to Curable, an online pain psychology program that uses modern technology to educate and guide individuals who've lived with any kind of lasting pain. Curable includes lessons, exercises, and a blog on pain and healing; articles on the most updated research on pain; testimonials; interviews with the leaders in the mind-body field; and a podcast of recovery stories.

For the next few weeks, I eagerly waited for each new podcast to post on the site. I took comfort in listening to the recovery stories of those with great physical and emotional pain. They inspired me and gave me hope. While each story and individual were unique, they were all eerily similar. And the best part was, they weren't scripted. They were raw and real!

During Dr. Stracks's class, he encouraged each of us to start a meditation practice. Becky had been trying to get me to meditate for some time, but I'd always resisted. I viewed meditation as having no role in healing. The cynic in me wondered, *Why would it? Why would thinking about nothing help?* I knew so little then. It still amazes me to look back and remember how close-minded I was then. I gave no thought to diving headfirst into any treatment a doctor would prescribe but automatically shut down other possibilities for healing that seemed to me too "out there." How was it that I'd immediately accepted terms from doctors like "spinal stenosis" and "stem cell injections" without a second thought or knowledge of what they meant, yet I dismissed practices such as "yoga" or "meditation" as silly or unhelpful?

Finally, after one day of being especially anxious, my body feeling as if it had been filled with a low-grade electrical vibration, I decided to take Dr. Stracks's advice and meditate. I heard him as if he were right there in the room with me: "Try to relax your nervous system."

Remembering what Dr. Stracks told me, I lay down in my dark bedroom and closed my eyes. Immediately, my heart began racing, my entire body felt hot, and sweat started beading on my forehead. I was scared shitless. Of what, I had no idea! To free myself of the anxiety, I opened my eyes, sat up, and wiped away the sweat.

Determined to follow my mentor's advice while wondering what had just hit me, I lay back down and, once again, I was only able to keep my eyes closed for ten or fifteen seconds before panic surged through my body. And then it hit me—I was afraid of the dark. What was I, seven years old?

Whatever was happening, it certainly wasn't relaxing or healing.

I decided to suspend my meditation practice, at least for a while.

CHAPTER 11

Surrendering

The rest of that fall continued to be a roller-coaster ride, both physically and emotionally. While hiking in the White Mountains of New Hampshire, I developed significant pain on the sides of both knees as soon as I started hiking downhill. I shared this with Dr. Stracks, and he was certain it was TMS. I had my doubts. I thought about the summer hikes we'd done in Wyoming. I did not have any issues with my knees then, but I also knew that hiking downhill could be a problem for people with arthritic knees. Perhaps that was me? Or was it TMS? Because I so desperately wanted a definitive answer to the cause of my pain, I tried to convince myself it was TMS.

On one hike, I spent two and half hours hiking up and felt really good, only to have my knees light up with pain after only 126 downhill steps. I knew it was 126 steps because I was curious how long it would take for the pain to appear, so I counted. I was always on the lookout for pain. Perhaps that was part of the problem—my intense focus on the problem, almost beckoning it to return, rather than concentrating on the beauty around me and everything I had to be grateful for each day. I was well aware of my tendency to focus on this pain, but I made no attempt to stop that behavior. At the time, I didn't know how. You can't simply tell someone who's anxious to stop feeling anxious. If it were that easy, no one would have any long-term anxiety! I can't tell you the number of people that told me I just needed to relax and not worry about the pain, but I never understood how it could be possible to turn the pain volume down. How could I heal when this fear was programmed so deeply into my cells? I needed tools. .

It was also on this hike, on the drive home, that I developed a ringing in my ears. Sometimes I'd experience tinnitus in my right ear but I'd always had it in my left ear. While I logically now knew my emotions were closely tied to my physical symptoms, I just couldn't relax when the symptoms appeared. While I still struggled seeing the connection between the two, I came to see that emotions and physical pain were tied together in a different way than what I had initially believed.

I had always assumed my emotions were a direct result of being in physical pain, and that certainly was the case at times. When I hurt physically, my mood would be affected, which made sense to me. I would be in pain and therefore miserable and depressed. But what I would eventually come to learn is that emotional pain is its own entity. Emotional pain can happen even in the absence of physical pain. (Some discovery, eh?) In fact, to take it a step further, I would discover that emotional pain often created physical pain— the exact opposite of what I'd always believed to be true.

Dr. Stracks's mind-body class turned out to be a good experience for me, and I looked forward to each weekly video conference call. I felt comfortable sharing my issues with the group and got relief during most of the calls, similar to the relief I achieved when working with Julie in PT. But we often talked about emotions on these calls: "What is your pain telling you? What are you experiencing emotionally when you have a spike in pain? When you have a spike in pain, sit with your pain and listen to what your body is saying."

I had a hard time relating to this. Truth be told, it seemed a bit silly. I didn't understand what Dr. Stracks meant when he said, "Pay attention to your emotions, particularly when you have a spike in pain." The spikes in pain I did have, such as when hiking downhill, I always attributed to a physical problem, not an emotional one. So, I thought there was no need to investigate that instance. I was looking for spikes in pain that I could tie to emotions, but they did not exist. Or so I thought.

At that time in my life, I was incapable of relating to my emotions. I had always held them back, although I didn't realize it then, so I waited in vain for an intrinsic message from my body. The one Dr. Stracks and others asked me to listen for. I simply figured that the people in the class who were tying pain to their emotions were making it all up. There was a young, single mother in the class who spoke of the onset of debilitating back pain. She believed it was her anxiety of having to take her young son on a camping trip for the weekend with the Boy Scouts. At the time, this made little sense to me. How could someone become anxious over camping? I couldn't think of a more relaxing activity. It took me a bit to recognize the obvious, that we're all wired differently. I'm sure some of my anxieties probably seemed strange to others, so I tried to shift my focus from judging to listening, and that in itself was healing—to be free of the negative energy of criticism.

I desperately wanted recovery and was hopeful this class would lead me to it. After five weeks of classes, however, I still didn't feel that journaling, meditating, or paying attention to my emotions was working. But, relentless in my desire to heal, I needed to take a closer look at my past—and present.

Dr. Stracks suggested I work with a therapist. He did not need to explain his reasoning to me. In *Healing Back Pain*, Sarno writes, "Although 95 percent of our patients heal themselves without psychotherapy, some will need such help. This means simply that they have higher levels of anxiety, anger, and other repressed feelings and that their brains are not going to give up this convenient strategy of hiding the feelings without a struggle."[9]

Without hesitation, I agreed to meet with a psychotherapist. That decision did not come without apprehension, but I was determined and committed to the process of healing, wherever that would take me. I clearly wasn't making any emotional breakthroughs on my own, and considering that was the basis of TMS, I knew I needed help. As much as I worried and obsessed over my pain, fortunately, my drive to free myself was stronger. After Dr. Stracks made an email introduction, I quickly made contact with Dr. Eric Sherman in New York City, and we scheduled two face-to-face appointments the first week of December. Dr. Sherman trained and worked directly under Dr. Sarno for many years, so he was familiar with TMS. Having very little idea what psychotherapy was, and how that could help with body pain, I sent him an email, asking how we would accomplish my goal of healing.

He responded: "One goal of treatment is to help you develop other ways of dealing with your feelings besides developing physical symptoms (TMS). Towards that end, we will work to help you identify your feelings and understand why certain feelings cannot be experienced directly as emotions, but instead need to be camouflaged as physical symptoms."

Damn . . . this was going to be heavy!

I had a few weeks to kill before I flew to Manhattan to meet with Dr. Sherman. After two days in New York, I would fly to Wyoming to try to capture some early-season skiing in the backcountry.

---

9   Sarno, *Healing Back Pain*, 101.

Knowing I was headed to Wyoming was always a source of comfort. In the days that led up to my visit with Dr. Sherman, Becky gave me a book she thought I might find interesting, *The Surrender Experiment* by Michael A. Singer. Singer's memoir tells the story of how he let go of personal fear and desires and allowed life to take its course naturally.

Singer, who went from being homeless to the head of a hugely successful company, wrote,

> Life rarely unfolds exactly as we want it to. And if we stop and think about it, that makes perfect sense. The scope of life is universal, and the fact that we are not actually in control of life's events should be self-evident. The universe has been around for 13.8 billion years, and the processes that determine the flow of life around us did not begin when we were born, nor will they end when we die. What manifests in front of us at any given moment is actually something truly extraordinary—it is the end result of all the forces that have been interacting together for billions of years. We are not responsible for even the tiniest fraction of what is manifesting around us. Nonetheless, we walk around constantly trying to control and determine what will happen in our lives. No wonder there's so much tension and anxiety and fear. Each of us actually believes that things should be the way we want them, instead of being the natural result of all the forces of creation.[10]

I thought long and hard about this passage as I moved through the first chapter. I'd understand it for a moment, only to lose it the next. I thought about all our ski trips to Wyoming and the angst I created in my mind—and body—over the weather and conditions, something that was clearly beyond my control.

I felt responsible when the conditions did not line up for friends

---

10   Michael A. Singer, *The Surrender Experiment* (New York: Harmony Books, 2015), 3–4.

and family. After reading his book, I was starting to see what a colossal waste of time that probably was. But what did it mean for everything else? Was Singer suggesting we just *go with the flow* and relinquish control over everything? Where did personal responsibility, effort to influence change, and moral decision-making come into play? I became confused and unsure how it might apply to my own life.

On December 10, 2018, which was around my two-year anniversary of living with chronic pain, I arrived in New York City. I immediately headed to 34th Street for my afternoon appointment with Dr. Sherman. Feeling nervous and unsure of myself, I stopped at his building's entrance and felt the towering presence of the Empire State Building looming from behind. I started to worry more and wondered if I would be lying on a couch as we talked. *Shit, I hope not*, I thought. It seemed cliché and felt like it would put me in such a vulnerable position.

My anxiety levels were starting to rise. I'd never spoken with anyone about my emotions before and I'd certainly never explored my past in therapy. This was as foreign to me as visiting the mountains and *not* wanting to hike or ski. Before I pushed through the revolving doors, I thought of *The Surrender Experiment* and told myself to stop thinking about what I wanted the appointment to look like and, instead, just experience it. Surrender.

It turned out there was no couch, just a regular old chair. And Dr. Sherman started by asking me to call him Eric, which immediately put me at ease. While Dr. Stracks was Midwestern friendly, Eric was a true New Yorker, loud and to the point. I appreciated the contrast in the two doctors.

After four hours of talking over a two-day period, Eric said that, in addition to my being a very intense guy, he thought that I'd been carrying a great deal of anxiety my whole life, and we'd work to release that in the coming months. He seemed confident that my underlying psychological issues were at the root of my physical pain. I didn't ask, but he told me I should expect at least six months of weekly calls before I saw any meaningful improvement in my symptoms. With all the stress and anxiety I had been experiencing over the last few years, I was a bit surprised that this timetable did not concern me . . . it was my very own surrender experiment!

I left the appointment feeling pretty good. I was one step closer to healing! By the time I got to the airport, something had changed. My mood had turned to sadness, the ringing in my ears was noticeably louder, my feet felt frozen. My arms and hands were riddled with tingling sensations from my biceps to my fingertips. I hadn't noticed these symptoms developing but suddenly, there they were. Not wanting to talk, I was at least able to text Becky while at the airport and even on the flight, which helped a great deal. As soon as I read her texts and connected with her, my worries started to decrease. The pain was still there, but it seemed less daunting with Becky on my side.

Back in Wyoming, I again picked up *The Surrender Experiment*. The more I read, the more I was moved by Singer's willingness to take what life brings. In a truly amazing sequence of events, he went from being a yogi living in the woods of Florida with no job to running a billion-dollar medical billing software company, to having that same company raided by the FBI and, ultimately, being prosecuted for fraud. The fraud was committed not by Singer, but rather a rogue employee, and the charges were eventually dropped. Throughout it all, Singer surrendered.

After reading more of *The Surrender Experiment*, I was suddenly overcome with the thought that maybe I could share my story to help others heal. I had something important to say. Perhaps there could be some good that would come out of my experience. Maybe I could spare others from the misery I'd been through.

Now, filled with a newfound purpose, I knew what I needed

to do. I could write a book. I was so excited. I jumped to my feet and sprinted across the condo and gazed out the window at the snow-covered mountains. The energy running through my body only allowed me to stay at the window for a moment before I sprinted back to where I had been sitting. Unable to sit at the computer, I ran back to the window with the excitement of a child on Christmas morning. That back and forth went on for fifteen minutes. When I was finally able to slow down, I said with a smile on my face, "I am going to write a book, holy shit."

And just as suddenly as I'd made the decision to write a book, doubt crept in. *Write a book, are you kidding me? You can't write a book. You barely graduated from high school and college. Plus, you stayed back in kindergarten. Who the F stays back in kindergarten?*

Because I'd been held back in kindergarten, I was always older than my classmates. And I carried that shame of repeating kindergarten all the way to high school . . . and beyond. I even chose not to get my driver's license when I was sixteen and waited an extra year. All in an attempt to protect myself from being exposed as older than everyone else. I slowly began to realize I had been spending an awful lot of energy hiding my insecurities from everyone and wondered if those actions had played a role in my ill health.

Then I had another about-face as I recalled my connection to *The Surrender Experiment.* Although my mind was telling me I was not good enough or capable of writing a book—that no one wanted to hear what I had to say—I reminded myself that in the short time since I'd picked up Singer's book, I'd been committed to my own surrender and accepting where the flow of life would take me—and the flow was to share my story.

CHAPTER 12

Meditation

As soon as I decided to write a book, I began to question the decision. My doubts about writing occurred in tandem with doubts about my diagnosis.

A few days before Christmas in Wyoming, I developed a sharp weight-bearing pain in my groin as I stood on my left leg putting my ski clothes on. I put it out of my mind, and we headed out to the mountain. But that day, anytime I looked over my right shoulder, my left hip would fire with sharp pain. All I could think about was what the hip surgeon had told me: my left hip would need to be replaced in two to four months. We were now at twenty months.

I visualized the ball of my femur being restricted by my hip socket as the pelvis rotated. Because a specific movement was causing the pain, surely it must be a physical cause and not TMS. Would I need a hip replacement after all?

I couldn't stop asking myself whether the pain was structural or TMS. That question created all sorts of anxiety.

In *The Surrender Experiment*, Singer states, "Challenging situations create the force needed to bring about change. The problem is that we generally use all the stirred-up energy intended to bring about change, to resist change."[11]

I decided to email Dr. Stracks and get his opinion on this groin and hip pain. As was customary, he promptly wrote back:

Hi, Mike.

I'd say for now, assume the hip is TMS. There's no urgency to it (no emergency hip replacements necessary!). So, you have time. Work to calm down your mind, calm down your brain, and assume it's just more of the pain moving around. There is always time to investigate further down the road, but treat it as TMS for now. Talk to your brain, be kind but firm.

And enjoy the holiday, the time with your children, the skiing, if you're in Wyoming, and all the hard work and progress you've made this year.

Happy Holidays,
Dr. Stracks

He was right. My mind had already been racing down the road toward another hip replacement. Had I learned nothing? It always shocked me how my mind could take over so quickly with concerns.

It was during this time I also recommitted myself to trying meditation to see if I could gain some traction with it. In addition to Becky's and Dr. Stracks's encouragement that I try meditation, I kept reading about it in the TMS research, and in other books and articles on pain management. Meditation seemed to be everywhere.

I decided a guided meditation would help keep me focused. Or

---

11   Singer, *The Surrender Experiment*, 160.

maybe distracted. A gentle voice and soft music relaxed me quickly, and soon I was able to meditate for ten to twenty minutes each morning. At first, I would meditate lying down, which was more comfortable for me. But I struggled to stay awake. I then switched to sitting with my legs crossed and my spine straight. Over the next month, I became very comfortable with the practice. Though I saw no immediate benefits in regard to my pain, I found the twenty minutes in meditation to be quite peaceful. I could feel the energy and tension normally racing through my body release when I meditated. My shoulders relaxed, my breathing slowed, and sometimes I would even feel tingling in my limbs. While I had no idea yet if the meditation practice would ultimately help my pain, I was confident from my body's reaction during meditation that it was a good thing. My body needed this.

Back in New Hampshire, I continued with my meditation practice, but the pattern of pain remained unchanged. It was not terrible, just an increase in the electric current in my feet and arms, a ringing in my ears, and a return of knee pain. Becoming increasingly anxious, verging on panic, I had growing concerns:

- Why have I seen an increase in pain since I have been home?
- Is it my expectation to have more pain when I'm home?
- Is it because I can't be as active in New Hampshire?
- Is it because I wish I was in Wyoming?

While working with Eric, he shared that he believed something happened in my childhood that I still carried with me. I'd always hoped that we would discover or discuss something vital in therapy, and I would be instantly healed. But so far, that big dramatic event had not occurred.

My recovery to this point was frustrating. I was told by Becky,

Dr. Stracks, and Eric how much better I seemed to be doing, but it didn't feel that way. It had been six months since I'd discovered TMS. I had seen a TMS doctor, taken a nine-week mind-body course, had done plenty of reading, and spent over two months in psychotherapy. I'd even begun meditating! And I had yet to recognize any sort of shift in my overall pain that would give me greater hope.

But that began to change during the middle of January. Jackson Hole was in the crosshairs of a pretty good storm cycle—one that could last a week. Even though I was experiencing pain in various areas, I was confident the pain would not slow me down, and I purchased an airline ticket on short notice. After three straight days of snow, the avalanche conditions in the backcountry became elevated and too dangerous, particularly when touring by myself. So I decided I would ski at the resort the next day. I arrived at the tram line at 7:00 a.m., so I could be first in line to the top of the mountain for the big powder day.

At 9:05 a.m. they loaded the first tram, and I was on it. The tram is a big red box that carries one hundred skiers, all standing, packed in like sardines. It's so tight, in fact, that there's hardly enough room to breathe. There is a lot of hooting and hollering on days like this, as the tram makes its fourteen-minute journey to the top. About halfway up, standing and unable to move, I noticed something unusual. With my goggles up, I realized I had my eyes closed, and I felt an amazing sense of calm. I was unaware of the growing excitement from my fellow skiers or their cheers. I was in a place of total peace. Both mind and body felt beautiful and perfect. I opened my eyes and felt as if I were invisible among the ninety-nine other skiers. Yet, as odd as it sounds, I also felt deeply connected to each of them.

My eyes were closed for over five minutes, but no one seemed to notice. Or they didn't care. Or maybe I didn't care. It did not take long for me to recognize the feeling—the same sensation I'd often gotten during my meditation at home, only better. No longer feeling self-conscious, I closed my eyes again for the remaining five minutes of the ride. As soon as my eyes closed, and with a deep cleansing breath, I was again taken over by the sense of calmness and connection to my body. It was an amazing moment—one of such clarity. I repeated that exercise every time I went up the tram that day. It was now clear to me that my meditation practice was starting to pay dividends. This was the first real sign of healing.

That experience did not change my physical pain. In fact, at the time, in typical fashion, my symptoms were very light because I was in the mountains. But even when I was feeling good physically, I always carried with me a sense of uneasiness, or of being on guard. It was subtle, but it was always there. But not this day, which was perfect!

About a month later, I experienced a similar meditative moment. This time, I was back home, sitting by myself and reading, when I noticed how calm I felt—much calmer than I had been in some time. I paused for a few moments to observe what was going on. Then I told myself my pain must have subsided to enable me to feel this calm. So, I took a quick inventory of my body. I was wrong. I still had the usual symptoms in my feet, hands, and arms, along with the ringing in my ears. *How could I be this calm with the many sensations I was feeling in my body?*

My first conclusion was that I must be sick and tired of worrying all the time about my pain. Perhaps it was just too draining. But after further reflection, I concluded it was the effects of my daily meditation practice. I immediately thought about Dr. Stracks. One of the first things he had recommended to me was that I try meditation to see if I could get my nervous system to relax.

I now recognize healing happens when we put in the work and create deep changes by connecting with our true self. Why had it taken me almost five months to fully grasp what he was saying? Unfortunately, the nervous system is not like an on/off switch, so it takes time. Regardless, I now understood what he meant. I was experiencing it. My pain was not different. It really had not improved. The cycle of pain was still in place, but I was at peace. I was the witness to my calm center.

It was the first time in many months, particularly when by myself, that I experienced physical pain or sensations but was able to remain relaxed and comfortable. Up to this point, anytime I had pain, I became tense and worried. It surprised me I could experience pain and ease at the same time. This was a foreign feeling for me. I was cautiously optimistic but had no idea what the next step in recovery would be, or if there would be another step.

I was just hoping it would continue.

CHAPTER 13

Psychotherapy

O ver the next several months, I finally decided to try to
focus more on my emotional healing and try not to pay
too much attention to the pain or sensations in my body.
After a lifetime of ignoring my feelings, I guess it had taken me a
bit longer than most to fully embrace this new path. For the most
part, my new focus worked; if I felt pain in my body, I tried not to
obsess over it. It was time to explore my emotional life, frozen for so
long. If I had TMS, then according to the theory, I had emotions I
wasn't allowing myself to feel, so that was being expressed through
the body. If I permitted myself to feel my emotions, then I'd experience less physical pain. I was willing to give it a try. What did I
have to lose?

I was eager to turn over any rock in my sessions with Eric that
might lead to healing. We conducted our weekly FaceTime sessions
on Tuesday mornings. While Eric was not into the outdoors like I
was, we often started each call talking about what I was up to in the
mountains. He seemed genuinely interested and quite amused with

it all. I was now fully committed to the healing process and very seldom did Eric need to tease something out of me. I still found it a bit awkward being so open, particularly with another male; it wasn't something I'd ever done with my father or brothers, and in my experience, my male interactions were much more superficial. But Eric never judged me and always put great value on what I had to say. Though I usually found some relief during the sessions, after each call I often felt unsure of myself, replaying the last hour in my mind and questioning how I did.

At times I would share with Becky what we'd discussed during the sessions, though I always took some time first to process what I'd discussed with Eric to feel comfortable sharing it. Becky had become better at giving me space to digest these powerful sessions. In time, I learned that Becky, independently, was actually going through her own work, giving up her belief that she was responsible for my healing. As a mom of three and living with someone with chronic pain, her instinct was to protect those around her and do everything she could to help. She now realized the most powerful way to help was to allow me to have space and time to heal.

Eric often commented on how brave and courageous I was. It was an odd comment, as I certainly did not feel brave. However, when I witnessed the type of healing work I was doing and thought of others doing the same, I recognized what a courageous effort it would be on their part. But I was just unable to see that it applied to me, as well. This was one of the first peeks I had into my history of low self-esteem. It was kindergarten all over again! Eric told me the idea of therapy is to understand what baggage you're carrying and learn to express it in other ways. Pain is present because there is something else you are not paying attention to.

At first, my work in therapy with Eric focused on my experiences as a student. It had always been clear to me that my time as a student had been challenging. From the time I was in kindergarten, school was a real hang-up for me. I was constantly petrified that I would be called on. I was always trying to make myself invisible.

I finally told Eric the kindergarten story. When I went to first grade, because my handwriting was so bad, they tried to change my dominant hand from left to right. After a few weeks they gave up, but they decided I was not ready for first grade and sent me back to kindergarten. To this day, I am still curious about what warranted that move. Struggling in school was always made worse by the fact that I was older than everyone in my class. I'd assumed you should be smarter if you were older and if you were not . . . well, you really had some issues.

A few years later, around the age of nine, I went to Massachusetts General Hospital in Boston with my father, where I was diagnosed with dyslexia. I don't recall any conversation about it, and I was left to figure out what it meant over the years. My father brought me to a couple of follow-up appointments, and I remember doing some hand-eye coordination exercises at home with my father. I even recall wearing glasses for a short time. However, the therapy quickly lost steam, glasses were lost, and it all just ended. I never learned what this diagnosis meant to me. It was similar to how every doctor who gave me a new pain diagnosis left me in the dark to struggle to find answers and meaning on my own. Or perhaps in both cases, I never absorbed what I was being told? And because of that, I drew my own conclusions: I was incomplete, limited in my abilities, and this needed to be hidden to prevent embarrassment.

What I thought of myself and what I thought to be true had far-reaching implications and seemed to get reinforced on a consistent basis. In fifth grade, we were taught how to write an outline. I was so nervous; it was all a blur to me. After a handful of lessons, we had an assignment to write an outline on our own. It was like I'd been absent from the previous four classes. I was paralyzed.

Somehow, I convinced a good friend to write the outline for

me. A few days later when our teacher made the rounds handing back the graded assignment, I was frozen in my seat, wondering if I would be busted for cheating, or worse, if a good friend would be in trouble. I held firmly on to my seat as she made her way to me. With a huge smile on her face, she put the assignment on my desk and on the top right corner in red ink was an A+. *Shit, that's way too obvious.* Mrs. Nelson kneeled down so we were eye level and told me how happy and proud she was of me. And she meant every word, I could tell.

"I *knew* you could do it!" she said, grinning.

But I did not do it. I felt terrible. I was just looking to get a passing grade to avoid the embarrassment of failing the assignment. But instead, I felt that familiar frozen feeling. There was no joy or relief from getting an A+, none whatsoever. Her big smile told me that she never believed I could do the work. And she was right.

A year later, in sixth grade, I broke my foot playing basketball, which required a cast and crutches. Our school was two stories with a sweet elevator. And since I was on crutches, I was permitted to use the elevator. That was a very big deal for a sixth grader. After the cast was removed, I was still using the crutches for a while, and, of course, the elevator. One day, as the elevator door was sliding closed, at the last second, a hand came in and stopped the door from closing. It was my sixth-grade teacher, Mr. Hanson, who I considered a good guy with a cool, well-trimmed beard. He looked pissed and his face was kind of red. He inched closer into my personal space and said quietly, with anger in his voice, "You're not hurt. You're a fraud. That's all you are is a fraud."

Motionless, I had no response. I stared at him, because that was all I could do. That only seemed to increase his anger, as though the big kid was staring him down. He stood his ground, waiting for me to respond. When I offered no rebuttal, he simply turned around and left me in the elevator alone. I tried to ignore the whole incident, as if it never happened, even though what he thought of me really bothered me. I never shared this story with any of my friends or parents. It never occurred to me to share it with anyone. That's not what I did as a kid. I kept everything bottled up inside. But I thought about it a lot for a long time, trying to figure out not why Mr. Hanson was such an asshole, but why I *was* still on crutches after I'd had the cast removed. I thought perhaps Mr. Hanson was right: I no longer needed the crutches or the elevator—I was milking the injury and I was a fraud. I had always liked and respected Mr. Hanson, and that made his opinion of me that much more painful.

After I told this story to Eric, he was disgusted with this teacher's behavior and told me that someone like that should not be influencing kids. Even if I had been milking the injury, that's not how you speak to a kid. He went on to explain that children think differently. They don't fully understand how the world works yet, interpreting situations through the eyes of a child, not an adult. A child would be unable to understand that maybe it was the teacher who had the issue. But the child (me) only heard that he was being called a fraud by an adult.

Even in church I felt as if I was being singled out as a fraud. While preparing for confirmation, we were required to fulfill a certain number of hours of community service over several months. No one ever asked me how I was doing with my community service, so in my typical fashion, it was somewhat out of sight, out of mind. I was unsure what to do, how to go about fulfilling the service hours, and maybe I was too scared or embarrassed to ask, silly as that sounds. The night before confirmation we had a rehearsal at the church. We lined up to make our way to the front of the church. Just before I got to the altar, someone grabbed my elbow and pulled me from the line. Not more than six feet from the rest of the class, I was told that because I did not fulfill my service hours, I would not be confirmed the next day and was asked to leave immediately. I remember looking over and making eye contact with a good friend. I could tell he felt bad for me. That eye contact was painful. I felt I had no one to blame but myself, and I walked home terribly upset and embarrassed.

Now I see it was times like those throughout my childhood that created my anxiety. And once that anxiety set in, I retreated inward, developing a habitual pattern of never learning how to communicate and express my feelings. These were breakthroughs for me. It suddenly became so clear how those moments impacted me for years to come without my knowledge.

Eric also spoke about the effects stress and anxiety have on a child's ability to learn. If a child is under enough stress, he explained, they can develop a wall of resistance, preventing them from absorbing information. I told him that is what it felt like for me in school. I would hear a teacher talking, but it felt like the information would evaporate as it hit my body. I think I was either too scared to learn or unable to focus, always fearful and on guard. I know the anxiety from the diagnosis of dyslexia played a role, probably more than the dyslexia itself. I even wondered sometimes if I really had dyslexia.

From first grade through twelfth grade, I only remember one class I took that was for students with learning problems, in ninth or tenth grade. There were only four students in the class, and the other three I would describe as having significant learning disabilities. I hated entering that classroom, fearing my friends would see me. I got good at sliding in without being seen. In the class, it was one-on-one teaching. And though I had many insecurities, I did feel safe and comfortable there, allowing myself to let down my guard, ask questions, and learn. Looking back at it now, it was a positive experience. Maybe I just needed a different way of learning, with or without dyslexia.

Eric told me how anxiety makes a child feel uncomfortable, which, in turn, has an adverse effect on how their memory works and their ability to process information. It can snowball and lead to children avoiding homework, not because they don't want to do it, but rather from the cascading effect anxiety has. All this results in falling behind in class, which then makes the anxiety about school even worse. Understanding how stress and anxiety can affect a child's ability to learn made a lot of sense to me and allowed me to start to fill in some of the gaps and answer questions about myself.

Maybe I wasn't such a dummy after all. I had carried that false belief around for fifty-two years. It made me wonder, *What other false beliefs am I carrying?*

CHAPTER 14

Family

As work with my therapist continued, we focused on my childhood. Eric believed my physical pain was there to help me avoid uncomfortable emotions from my past. He suggested the physical symptoms protected me from experiencing strong emotions. My question was always the same: What are those emotions and where did they come from?

And he'd remind me, "Most often your emotions are heavily influenced by childhood experiences."

I described my childhood beyond the kindergarten trauma as best I could. I had many good memories of being a kid. I had a lot of friends and I enjoyed sports and all the typical after-school activities associated with being a boy. Our family owned a chalet in the White Mountains of New Hampshire, where we would spend weekends skiing in the winter. And during the summer months, we would spend time on the lakes and rivers. This is where I developed my passion for the outdoors, as did my two older brothers. To this day, every time I walk along a stream in Wyoming, I am immediately brought back to times we walked along the small babbling brooks behind our chalet in the White Mountains. It's a good feeling and the connection is deep.

I was the second to youngest of five children. I had two brothers—six and eight years older than me—and two sisters, one five years older and one a year younger.

My mother, Nan, was great. She had a youthful spirit and her intelligence was sneaky smart! I remember her taking me and a couple of my friends to a Red Sox game for my tenth birthday. In fact, while my father always secured the tickets to games, it was always my mother who brought me. That evening, there was a lengthy rain delay, and I don't think the game got started until close to midnight. While most people left, we remained. I remember running around Fenway Park with my buddies in the rain on a warm summer night, looking up underneath the roof where my mother sat to stay dry. She would toss a fun smile our way, essentially giving us the green light to continue with what we were doing. It was so much fun!

My mother loved Christmas, and she loved to shop. The room where we put our Christmas tree every year would overflow with perfectly wrapped presents. Decorating the Christmas tree was always a big deal for her. She would have us thread real popcorn with a needle to make the decorations as authentic as possible. Some years, our tree had all white lights; other years there were big colored lights, with lots of tinsel.

As a town selectman, my father, Jack, was involved with politics. He volunteered a lot of his time to the town in all sorts of ways. He sold cement in Boston and this job afforded him a lot of flexibility, so he was often around the house.

He was a big man, six foot three, with a large frame and big, meaty forearms. My father loved the Red Sox and the TV shows *All in the Family* and *Barney Miller*. I think I was too young to understand *All in the Family* and Archie Bunker's humor. But I did get a kick out of hearing his deep laugh as he watched the show from his comfortable La-Z-Boy recliner.

He enjoyed going to the supermarket, for anything. I swear he would forget something just to be able to run back out. And he was always willing to strip a ten or twenty out of his wad of cash for his kids—always!

My father loved to feed me and my friends: late-night pancakes, French toast, or his famous and often undercooked BBQ wings. He took great interest in my sports in high school, both football and lacrosse. I knew he enjoyed watching me compete and he missed very few games. Reflecting on my kids and the joy I received from watching them on the field, I gained a better understanding of what he was experiencing. I am thankful for his support and glad that I was able to provide some joy in his life. He passed away too young, at the age of seventy-two from heart disease. I am glad he'd been able to meet Mikey and Kaylee.

My father also had a short temper that got the better of him often. It was scary when he lost it. But there was no question in my mind about the love he had for me and our family. When he retired from town politics, they had a party for him. I remember one of the things they said about him: "Jack Murray, family, town, and job. That's what is important to him—in that order." I would have to agree with that. I remember feeling incredibly proud of my father that evening, to hear the town officials speak so glowingly of him. I was many years away from even thinking about having kids, but it occurred to me that *family first* felt right.

I began to realize while talking with Eric that my father's explosive temper seemed normal to me. When I was probably around eight years old, my younger sister and I were going to the store with our father. We were sitting in the backseat as he drove down a main road. I could hear a horn aggressively honking at us from behind. It became very apparent that whoever was behind us was not happy with my father's driving, though I didn't recall my father cutting anyone off. The honking went on for a minute or so and while no words were spoken between the three of us, you could feel the tension in our car increase.

At some point, this car passed us and the driver tossed my father the middle finger. As the man pulled in front of us, he slammed on his brakes only to increase his speed moments later. Still no words were spoken in our vehicle. Soon after, the traffic light turned red and the guy was forced to stop, with us behind him.

The driver jumped out of his car with his arms waving in our direction and a cigarette butt hanging out of his mouth. As fast as this guy got out of his car, my father hopped out of ours faster. My father closed the gap between the two of them with surprising speed. In a blink of an eye, my father had one hand wrapped around the man's neck with his thumb buried deep into his larynx, while my father's other fist was raised, ready to land a punch. This fellow picked the wrong guy to mess with.

With the front door still open from my father's quick exit, I was able to make out a handful of words: "Get back in your fucking car," my father said, "or I'll stuff you under your hood." That was no idle threat. I knew it, my sister knew it, and the guy knew it. The driver nodded and my father released him from the death grip, allowing him to breathe again. It all happened so fast. When my father got back in the car, he did not utter a word about what had just happened—it was as if we were not even there—but I certainly felt the tension. Part of me was impressed by my father's dominance, but I was also scared and unsure about what to do. While the event itself was certainly traumatic, I realize now I was more concerned about his absolute silence during the car ride afterward.

When my father was in a bad mood, it was no fun to be around him. When I was in elementary school, my parents put in a backyard pool. I have some great memories of us hanging out in the pool area during the day and more so at night as I got older. However, the weekly cleaning of the pool was a completely different matter. I'm sure each of my brothers and sisters also had the unfortunate task of helping my father vacuum the pool. It was awful.

The pool filter was located in the back of the garage and getting to it was not a simple task. Our garage was always a mess, which only added to my father's stress level. It seemed we always had a problem with our filter, and my father's idea of a toolbox was a hammer. If something didn't fit, he'd just pound at it until it did. At the first sign of a problem, he was like a teakettle blowing off steam.

My father often told us he didn't swear, or he would say, "You don't hear me using language like that." That was true, unless, of course, he lost his cool, in which case he would swear *a lot*. A short, powerful burst of "Jesus Christ" was his go-to, but he was also not opposed to dropping the F-bomb. At some point in the pool-cleaning process, I'd be asked to operate the switch that would send electricity to the filter. I'd wait for his command and each time I would throw the switch and sparks would fly from the panel. It was terrifying, but he did not seem the least bit concerned with the electrical problems. Between my father's anger and the sparks flying, the weekly pool cleaning pretty much sucked. Once the filter was ready, the vacuuming would commence. This part of the job was no better. It got to the point where I was just waiting for him to lose his cool for whatever reason. There were never any laughs while doing this work, and there could have been, there should have been.

While cleaning the pool was always difficult, at least I knew what to expect and could mentally prepare myself. But my father's unexpected rages were the source of my greatest stress. For example, during seventh-grade football, my father offered to help, making him one of five coaches. I don't recall being concerned about his temper. I think I was just happy he was out on the field with us; with him there, I felt a sense of belonging and connection.

One game, in particular, stands out in my memory. We were on defense. It was third down and the offense had two yards to go for a first down. The opposing team ran the ball up the middle and got the first down. In anger, I kicked the dirt and unwittingly kicked dirt in the running back's face who was still lying on the ground. The referee quickly threw a yellow flag and I was penalized with a fifteen-yard unsportsmanlike play. Still unsure of what I'd done, I was immediately taken out of the game.

As I jogged off the field, still wondering what the penalty was for, our head coach made his way toward me. He was one of the best coaches I'd ever had. While he was a yeller and could get very mad, he was also caring. He often pushed the envelope with his shouting, but I loved his intensity and thrived under his coaching style. My father once told me that if the coach was not yelling at you, he didn't care about you.

As I jogged directly toward my head coach, out of nowhere, my father ran over to us and started losing his shit. He was verbally leaning into me, and hard. It didn't take long to understand I had kicked dirt in the kid's face and he thought I had done it on purpose. As my father continued yelling in my face, I could see my head coach out of the corner of my eye yield and walk away. I was unable to get a word in—even if I'd had a chance to take out my mouth guard—and tell my father it was an accident. Standing on the field, I simply stood there and let my father dish it out.

After what seemed like several minutes of yelling, I gave up trying to explain myself, embarrassed for both of us. I walked around my father to our sideline with the rest of the team. But he followed me, still shouting, as I tried to lose him among my teammates. I couldn't believe what was happening. I kept walking, my back to him, past the other players. I just wanted him to stop but knew better than to say another word.

As my father continued to direct his rage toward me, I became numb. It was a coping strategy I guess I'd developed at an early age to shield myself from his moments of anger. While the head coach would yell at me, he had a good reason and there was always a coaching moment attached to it. My father, however, simply lost control on the field. There was no constructive criticism or explanation of why he was so furious with me. To this day, the whole scene baffles me.

My father and I didn't talk about it on the drive home. And I don't remember who took me to my next practice. What I do remember is my head coach running over as soon as I got to the field. Even as a young kid, I could tell he'd been waiting for me. With no one around, he took his ball cap off, dropped his head slightly, and told me that he understood that I did not purposely kick dirt in the opposing player's face, and he said he was sorry for the incident. He was very sincere, and it felt good to be validated like that. But there was no reason for him to apologize. It seemed like he was apologizing for my father's behavior. From that moment, my respect for the coach grew even greater. As with other outbursts, my father never showed remorse or acknowledged the incident. I even questioned my own memory and wondered if I'd just imagined the whole thing. But recently, when speaking with my older brother, I learned that my father had shared the story with him. But for whatever reason, he was uncomfortable discussing it with me. Perhaps this was his way of working through his guilt.

While thinking about those key incidents in my sessions with Eric, I was able to understand how I learned to shut down and ride out my father's anger. Other children may have had the choice to speak up and show some emotion. But I had no idea how to do that. It was simply not part of my emotional toolbox back then.

As Eric listened to my stories, he introduced me to the concept of childhood trauma. I struggled to understand how it related to me. I was not subjected to physical abuse. We did not have physical violence in the home. There was no divorce. All in all, it seemed pretty normal. But what I began to learn in these sessions is, a child does not have to be exposed to extreme traumatic events, such as sexual abuse, physical abuse, or drug or alcohol addictions to experience trauma in the body.

In fact, a child's brain is unable to tell the difference in traumatic events. Stress is stress. And the more often a child experiences stress, the greater the impact. I learned that early childhood trauma can be especially harmful, as a child's brain grows rapidly, particularly during the first few years. Trauma can be as much about what the child did *not* get. Sometimes parents are not able to give the emotional support the child needs, such as love, affection, and physical contact.

I had many positive memories growing up, and I knew my parents had done the best they could. In many ways, I had a very lucky and sheltered childhood. But I'd grown up in a stressful home, and I carried that stress with me, unable to process it for the first time until my fifties. For some reason, it had never dawned on me that a household that was prone to unpredictable yelling and anger could have a massive effect on children. I'd always viewed childhood trauma through the lens of physical violence. I couldn't personally check that box, so therefore, I was in the clear. It amazed me that it took almost five decades to realize that my stress and anxiety were born from growing up in an atmosphere of stress and anxiety.

While doing my own inner work with Eric, I often wondered how many other people around the world might be carrying stress from their childhood. Perhaps, like me and not knowing the more subtle reaches of childhood trauma—far beyond the physical—they hadn't yet processed emotions that were manifesting themselves as physical pain, addictions, anger, anxiety, or depression.

CHAPTER 15

Triggered

B y now I had a couple of treatment techniques in play. Meditation was clearly helping, or at least helping to keep me
calmer. And I was starting to see that maybe my childhood
had played a role in my pain. But it was not as though I'd uncovered
some deep, forgotten experience from childhood. The vast majority
of these memories had been readily available to me. Yet now, looking back and by working with Eric, I was intellectually starting to
see the possible connection between my repressed emotions and my
pain. So far, however, recognizing those events and emotions wasn't
providing any real relief from my constant physical or emotional
pain. And on some days, the whole path seemed pretty far-fetched,
even to me. But I kept going. I had to.

Since I'd discovered the mind-body connection almost eight
months prior, I had, like a lot of people with TMS, become obsessed
with learning as much as I could about the syndrome. Over the last
few months, I'd expanded my reading beyond TMS-specific books

to include spiritual readings: books on yoga, meditation, mind-body healing, stress management, and the effect of trauma on emotions. I even read a book on childhood emotional neglect, one about breathing, and another called *Romancing the Shadow* that draws on the teachings of the Swiss psychiatrist Carl Jung. While they were all different, and few ever mentioned Dr. Sarno and TMS, they all spoke about the effects repressed emotions have on the mind and body.

In my therapy sessions and through reading these books, I learned that emotions could get stuck in your body. And until you can release that emotion and experience, you will be susceptible to physical or emotional suffering, or maybe both. Though I hadn't seen real healing yet, everything I'd read and all the work I'd been doing with Eric convinced me that I was on to something and that I should continue down this path, however bizarre that course seemed to be.

I found great comfort in every book, podcast, and documentary that touched on this concept, particularly the ones that were not about TMS, because those showed me this was a real affliction that a huge percentage of the population was dealing with, and I was just one of many. In fact, as time went on, it became abundantly clear that few people escaped the effects of trauma and the emotional and physical pain that can accompany it.

In addition to my daily ten to twenty minutes of guided mindfulness meditation, I added *coherent breathing* to my routine. Every day, we breathe without giving it much consideration. But by controlling our breath, we can affect our body in a positive way. During my practice, I would sit quietly, slow my breath, and with the help of a cue from a YouTube video, I'd breathe four breaths per minute for ten minutes.

Breathing is part of the autonomic nervous system (ANS), which also includes your heart rate and digestion. If you can get your breathing to leave a stressed state, the rest of your ANS will follow suit. Deep breathing like this is an effective tool and an easy way to reduce stress and anxiety. It was during these breathing exercises that I was starting to tune in to my body and the subtle changes that can happen based on changes in the external environment. For example, while doing this very slow breathing exercise, I noticed I would struggle, at times, to maintain a clean, even breath. There were times when I felt I could not fully catch my breath. And times when it felt choppy. I finally recognized that whenever I struggled, I'd been doing the coherent breathing exercise upstairs. Could the simple task of walking up a flight of stairs be enough to affect the quality of my breath? Was this a dramatic finding? Hardly. But for me it was a sign of body awareness. Something that over time I would learn was important.

My weekly calls with Eric were surprisingly comfortable. I eagerly awaited each call in hopes of more healing. Because of my drive to heal, I was eager to share with Eric anything that might provide insight into my suffering: stressful times at school, dealing with my father's rage, or my low self-esteem. He would calmly listen, asking questions to keep me engaged, and when I was done, he would always say, "Mike, how did that make you feel?"

I still felt frozen whenever he'd ask that question, continuing to struggle with identifying my past feelings. Or any feelings for that matter. I would be unable to offer any type of coherent response. Dropping my head in disgust, I would remain silent. Looking back at it today, in addition to being unable to identify with my emotions, I was afraid of making a mistake and giving Eric the wrong answer. My low self-esteem was rearing its ugly head. The longer I struggled to come up with an answer, the greater my anxiety became. Thankfully, Eric had a way of making a seamless transition out of these awkward moments.

During our sessions, I learned that I had a pretty shallow understanding of my feelings. I could identify whether I was in a good or bad mood and that was about it. Toward the end of every call, Eric would encourage me to pay close attention to my emotions and my reactions, along with any increase in pain tied to them.

Pay attention to my emotions? I had zero idea how to do that. I'd spent my entire life ignoring my emotions. And it is so obvious to me now. I mean, I knew I had heavy anxiety and fear, but I had no idea if the pain created the anxiety and fear, or if the fear and anxiety created the pain. Were fear and anxiety other symptoms, just like nerve pain?

I still wasn't sure, but that all started to change one day in April 2019.

That afternoon, Jaimie had her first lacrosse scrimmage of her sophomore year. My symptoms that day were pretty light. I still had ringing in my ears, but the pain in my arms and legs was very low.

When the team took the field to start the game, they had Jaimie starting at midfield. Jaimie had excellent stick skills and was a great passer with good field vision, but she lacked speed, like most of the Murrays. Not long into the game, the coach removed Jaimie. A few minutes went by and she still had not been put back in. Standing by myself, I could feel my anxiety start to increase. I kept a close eye on Jaimie and the coach. Each time the coach passed Jaimie standing on the sideline, I wondered if she would give my daughter a tap on the shoulder and tell her to get back in the game.

I was no longer enjoying myself. Instead, I was feeling terrible for Jaimie. I've always wanted my kids to be happy and I struggle when they are disappointed (or I perceive they are disappointed). Every second that went by, I became more uncomfortable. I was not mad at the coach. This was a scrimmage, and she was just trying out different players. But I hurt badly for Jaimie. While she was not the best player, without question she was a key player and would start every game in the regular season. I knew this.

Even though I had a complete understanding of what was going on, I was unable to escape the negative feelings that were surfacing and getting stronger with every passing moment. All of a sudden, I realized my feet had become frozen in pain. Take the coldest mountain stream or cold ocean water and stand in it for twenty minutes and that's how my feet felt. Except I was not standing in ice cold water. It was fifty-five degrees outside. In this brief time, I had been affected emotionally, followed by the physical pain of frozen feet. A clear connection!

I tried to continue to watch, but I could no longer take the discomfort and watched the remainder of the game from my car. After the game, Jaimie jumped into the car with me. She didn't seem particularly upset with how the game went, but I was still feeling the effects, both physically and emotionally. I held the steering wheel firmly for the twenty-five-minute drive home while Jaimie sat silently doing some homework. I was filled with negative, explosive energy.

The remainder of the evening, the pain was still significant, but over the next twenty-four hours it slowly subsided to only light sensations. I was confused as to what had happened. Could my emotion over my daughter's lacrosse game, something that didn't even bother her, really have brought on that much physical pain? Once the pain was gone, I put the whole incident out of my mind, happy to be moving forward.

However, two days later, while sitting on our back porch, I received a text message from an old friend. After exchanging a few messages, he wrote something that set me off, and I felt a loss of breath and pressure in my head, as anger and resentment quickly invaded my body. Unable to let the innocent remark go, I began to create a story in my mind about the true meaning of his comment. Making no attempt to let the remark go, I did the opposite and was feeding off the negative emotions, allowing them to grow stronger and stronger while they began to occupy more of my mind. Looking back, I see how this loss of control so closely resembled my father.

As this was happening, I understood that the behavior and feeling were nothing new to me. I considered myself to be a happy person. I have a great family and a bunch of friends. I truly enjoy life. But it is not unusual for something to set me off, and I can quickly get myself all wound up with frustration or anger. You could even say I enjoyed those moments, since I did nothing to stop them and even sometimes relished the misery, replaying incidents over and over in my mind like a struggling drug addict.

That afternoon, sitting in the sun on our back porch reading the text message over and over, I noticed that I had developed significant pain, yet again. This time not only were my feet frozen, but my shins and knees had hot spots all over them. I compared the pain to the episode I'd had two days earlier at Jaimie's lacrosse game. And for the first time I understood, as it was happening, that I had been triggered. I had been upset at Jaimie's game and my feet became frozen. And now, I'd gotten upset at an old friend over an innocent comment, and I felt pain across my whole body. Emotional angst had been followed by a significant spike in physical pain.

I quickly thought about what Dr. Stracks had asked during our mind-body class: "What are you feeling right before you have a spike in pain? What is your pain telling you? What is the meaning of your pain?" And then I thought of Eric's advice and questions during our weekly calls: "Pay attention to your emotions and reactions. What do you see and feel? Only pay close attention to a meaningful increase or decrease in pain, or if your pain moves around. Next time you feel angry or threatened, pay attention to your heart rate and your pulse."

For months, I had felt Eric and Dr. Stracks were speaking a different language. I hadn't understood what they were saying. I couldn't make any of the connections they were looking for. But now that had changed. For the first time in almost two years of chronic pain I was able to tie emotions to what I was feeling in my body (my pain-body) and to a spike in pain. Whenever I was asked what I was feeling in my body when triggered, I always assumed they were talking about physical pain or emotional struggles. And those were certainly things to be on the lookout for. But something else happens in the body before the emotional reaction and physical pain take over. You need a certain kind of awareness to witness and *feel* what is happening inside your body. My daily meditation practice of almost eight months had cultivated that greater body awareness, and I now felt those shifts take place. The shifts preceded any emotional reaction and any physical spike in pain. It was as if my body was warning me before my mind was able to. The shifts that occur are most likely unique to each of us. They could range from an increased heart rate, a warm face, shortness of breath, or even a sense of external pressure.

While I had felt empowered by being able to make this connection, I'd wondered what the hell had taken me so long. *Was this all just part of my imagination?* It seemed to border on black magic for me.

During our next FaceTime call, I excitedly shared my story with Eric. With a big smile on his face, Eric congratulated me and added, "Not bad for a dumb kid." I understood the reference to how I had viewed myself throughout life. It was an exciting moment. But I had not yet found my holy grail—I was still in pain. While I recognized and noticed the onset of pain, that awareness had not alleviated the physical pain itself.

But I knew it was imperative that I stay the course and trust the process, and that was not always easy. I felt as if I was walking a narrow path blindfolded, unsure if I would be tripped up along the way. This clearly was a milestone for me, as were my experiences with the effects of meditation. But I had no strong indications of when or if there would be another step toward healing. It was like touring the backcountry of Wyoming during heavy snowfall with limited visibility. I was not one hundred percent confident I was heading in the right direction, but confident enough to keep moving forward in that same direction.

Discovering my feelings through those two triggered events was a real eye-opener for me. I was surprised by the depth and layers of my emotions. Since I was a kid, apparently, I'd learned to stuff my feelings down. But here I was exploring my feelings and the effects they had on my body. In the past when I had an experience like this—and there were plenty, trust me—all I understood was that I was furious or upset. I did not know there was more depth to the feeling. I would just sit with that anger until it left me. That could be minutes, hours, or days. I never understood my anger and rage, not that I tried to understand it or even think it unusual. I was oblivious to the impact of my feelings.

Now, as my awakening was taking place, I was able to look deeper. I did not have all the answers, but the first step seemed to be awareness. I was unable to acknowledge the negative emotions of hurt and sadness I had for Jaimie. They got stacked up inside of me and I could feel changes happening in my body. My breath would become shallow, and I could feel the pressure in my chest, neck, and head increase. That would quickly lead to emotional angst. Ultimately all this energy would pour out of my body through physical pain: frozen feet, ringing in my ears, and tingling sensations up and down my arms. As Dr. Sarno theorized, all that pain was designed to distract me from my emotional wounds. There were events that would trigger these wounds, and that is when my emotions went into overdrive, resulting in physical pain.

It now had been almost a year since my TMS discovery. I had a tendency to look at my recovery in a static way: *I feel good today, therefore I am improving. Or, I feel like shit, so I am getting worse.* It was often that black-and-white for me. I've since learned this is a common experience among those with chronic physical and emotional pain. Pain has a way of becoming all-consuming; it's easy to fall into the pain trap. When I expressed these concerns, Eric cautioned me not to think that and to understand there will be good days and bad days and that recovery was not a straight line. The trends were what mattered. But when you're in the thick of it, that can be tough to do.

The Power of Emotions

I began to have a better understanding of what was happening in my body and the potential path to healing. While I did not know why I was hit with the original hamstring and shoulder pain two years before, I now knew that once those TMS symptoms occurred, I became fearful and anxious, which engaged my fight-or-flight stress response.

Imagine being chased by a woolly mammoth; our fight-or-flight response is activated and readies us for battle (fight) or to run away from danger (flight). It does that by releasing chemicals like adrenaline into the body. This causes rapid heartbeat, shallow, rapid breathing, and tense muscles.

It's truly a remarkable system and was designed for our survival. However, I learned that living in this state over longer periods of time can have adverse effects on our physical health, such as widespread pain, fatigue, and digestive problems. I was intrigued when I learned the fight-or-flight system does not know the difference between an actual threat and a perceived threat—fearful thoughts where no real danger exists. And triggers are an individual thing. What you may see as a threat, I may find exciting, and vice versa. After learning this, I realized I'd been living in a semipermanent fight-or-flight state where no real danger existed. And now that I knew what was going on and why it was happening (childhood trauma), I could start to roll up my sleeves and do the work.

Through meditation, I'd been able to calm my entire nervous system, which, in turn, had slowly begun to reduce the pain and sensations I was having. With the reduction in pain, I was finally able to recognize the spikes in pain that everyone was asking me about.

And once I was able to see the spikes in my pain, I was able to identify the trigger. I would experience that trigger inside my body, which would then set off the emotions, followed by the physical pain—pain I would feel immediately or that took hours to appear. But now with my nervous system coming into balance, the spikes in pain became less frequent. Thankfully, these spikes were also not quite as severe, and did not last as long. But this was just the beginning of my healing journey.

Yes, I was starting to see *what* was setting me off (my triggers). The next step, I assumed, was learning *why*. My hope was that I'd eliminate those moments altogether, once I'd learned the triggers and why they affected me.

Unfortunately, I still had a black-and-white mindset. If I had any pain, I would immediately question my healing. My emotions when pain occurred were volatile (as modeled by my father). And I still often wondered whether all the pain stemmed from a structural issue.

Looking back, I think I should have given myself more credit for the healing that had taken place. During times of low pain, I would often talk to myself about how strong I was going to be emotionally during the next spike in pain. When it had been a few months since I weakened the pain cycle, I was confident that the spikes in pain would last only a few days and I would be able to stay positive during these spikes and ride them out emotionally. As I was learning, though, you can't consciously heal. Don't get me wrong. Awareness is critical, but true healing comes from the unconscious.

While I had been making some progress, as the 2019 Memorial Day weekend approached, I was still careful when and with whom I socialized. The last thing I wanted was to commit to doing something, only to feel blue that day and regret signing up for the night out. Feeling pretty good about things the Thursday before the holiday weekend, I sent out a few messages to friends, but everyone was busy. This was really no surprise, as most people don't wait until twenty-four hours before a long weekend to make plans. Having no plans was fine by me, but I did feel bad for Becky. She would have enjoyed hanging out with some of our friends, but she was cool about it and was looking forward to hanging out at the beach with me.

When we arrived on Friday, it was a beautiful day with some little waves. She encouraged me to grab my stand-up paddleboard to catch some waves while we were at the beach. The little waves turned out to be bigger than we'd originally estimated. It had been some time since I had been on a paddleboard surfing, but it didn't take me long to get back in the groove. For an hour or so, I had the surf break to myself, a rarity for that location, enjoying wave after wave in really fun surf conditions. It's amazing how nothing else exists when you're on a wave. It may last for only ten seconds, but during that time you're about as free as can be. And only that moment exists!

Later that day, we were back at the house enjoying the late afternoon sun on our back porch. When I got up, I felt a sharp pain in my left groin. Unlike the prior episodes of groin pain, this was constant. My mind immediately went to the arthritis in the left hip. *Shit!*

The pain took the wind out of my proverbial sails pretty quickly. I tried to keep a smile on my face for Becky. But inside I could feel the familiar angst developing. It was amazing how each spike in pain immediately led me down a dark path. I'd made so much progress, yet here I was, despite my best efforts, unable to stay calm and fully accept the pain as a mind-body condition. I couldn't understand, after being fully committed to this type of emotional healing for physical pain, how everything could fall apart so easily. Intellectually, I knew what I was supposed to do, but the old triggers and patterns of fear won out.

I know seeing the arthritis on the X-ray of my left hip played a role in triggering me. And while Dr. Stracks had told me after a previous spike in groin pain that it was most likely TMS, he never said I wouldn't need a second hip replacement. And while Sarno and the TMS community believed there were far too many unnecessary surgeries, they did not completely rule out the need for joint replacements, when warranted. I remember reading Sarno's book, in which he wrote about hip pain and replacements. He said that full hip replacements are one of the great achievements of reconstructive surgery. But he followed that up with, "One must, however, be very careful, for I have seen a number of patients whose hip pain was clearly due to a manifestation of TMS."[12]

Talk about a dilemma!

I told Becky about the groin pain, and she said, "You probably tweaked it during your paddleboard session."

I took a deep breath. It irked me when Becky would suggest the cause of my pain was physical activity or an acute injury. Never TMS. I would eventually come to see that this negative reaction I had to Becky's attempt to help was deep within me, making me feel as if I was not being heard, understood, or seen. Just like my experience with all the doctors, or with friends saying it was all about my age, or when my teachers made assumptions about me faking my broken leg.

---

12 Sarno, *Healing Back Pain*, 134.

Call it instinct or call it intuition, but I had come to know my body very well, and I knew that this groin pain was not an acute injury—not a pulled muscle, bad bruise, or strained ligament from surfing that day.

I spent the next day reflecting on my left groin pain, trying to tie a trigger to the spike. Was there an emotional connection? I started to think about the days prior to the onset of the groin pain. It didn't take me long to recognize that I'd been holding in guilt about my lack of weekend plans. It took some reflecting for me to see that the guilt I was carrying was significant and occupying space in my mind. I felt like I was letting Becky down and being selfish by not reaching out to our friends sooner. She deserved more.

Guilt, like any feeling, is normal. But you need to be able to process those feelings and allow them to pass through you. This was not happening with me; I was holding on to the guilt and beating myself up, unable to let go and experience my emotions.

As Sarno claimed, pain is designed to distract from emotional trouble. Steven Ray Ozanich writes in *The Great Pain Deception*, "TMS symptoms are a kind of slap to the back of the head to say, 'wake up, you're not truly happy with your situation.'"[13]

Once I realized guilt was the cause of my new groin pain, I decided to open up to Becky and share my feelings with her. I was embarrassed expressing this, and it required some blind faith on my part. But if confession is good for the soul, maybe it would free me of my physical suffering, too.

I looked over at her, reading the paper, and said, "This new groin pain is from my guilt over us not doing anything this weekend. I know how much you like to meet friends on the beach or go out,

---

13   Steven Ray Ozanich, *The Great Pain Deception* (Warren, Ohio: Silver Cord Records, 2011), 5.

and I feel bad about feeling selfish and not asking anyone sooner. I think this led to pain in my body."

A look of relief washed across Becky's face after I opened up to her. She smiled. "I just want us to be happy and for you to feel better. I only want to hang out with *you* this weekend. Not being around other people never even entered my mind as an issue."

We continued to talk about the guilt I felt and its effects.

"So your emotions play a *huge* role in how you feel," she said. "Crazy how holding on to your guilty feelings can actually result in pain! I don't really understand the whys of it all, but I get you now."

I felt more connected to Becky than ever before. I'm happy to report that the pain subsided within a couple of days and our relationship grew even deeper.

Seeing my emotions clearly and how they were affecting my body and my mind led me to rethink my past. I considered how often—an endless number of incidents—I became upset or angry only to keep it all bottled up inside of me, creating tension.

I thought about Dr. Stracks's comment when I first met him: "Maybe, Mike, you will need to take it easy on yourself." I'd felt threatened by that comment and always assumed he meant physically. I thought he was saying I shouldn't ski or take long bike rides anymore. Looking back, I sense he meant something else. I'd always known you could be too hard on yourself physically, but I'd never considered that could happen emotionally, too. Never in a million years had I thought I was hard on myself. But as I was becoming aware of my emotional triggers, I was understanding the unnecessary tension I'd held in my body over a long period of time. It was how I operated.

As I continued on this path of discovery and healing, I was always shocked by how often I'd been protective of my past behavior. If only someone had whispered in my ear, "Hey, Mike, what you think about yourself might not be true, and you may be doing harm to your body with all of your misguided beliefs." Just once.

With my slow awakening, I was more cognizant of how I was feeling and reacting. This type of healing does not happen overnight. It is hard work that is part of a long, slow process with many setbacks. But I kept at it.

One Saturday afternoon I decided to jump on my road bike and head out for a ride. After about ten miles, I headed to a neighborhood where my good friend Chad lives with his wife, Kerri. When I was still working, they were two of my top sales performers. They'd met at the office and married. As I approached the cul-de-sac where they lived, not only were Chad and Kerri outside, but they were setting up for a block party and a few of their friends had already arrived. There were a half dozen coolers—surely packed with beer—and a grill and table with covered food, waiting for more people to arrive.

It was nice to see them both as we talked and caught up. After about ten minutes, Kerri motioned to some of her friends to come over.

"Guys, this is Mike Murray. He was the president of our company and is responsible for Chad and I having been able to buy our beautiful house."

She said those words with a kind smile on her face, yet I felt as if I'd gotten punched in the stomach, and I had shortness of breath. I had always been uncomfortable with compliments, particularly when it came to business. Now with my lens of new awareness, I felt the emotion impacting me in real time.

The seconds after her kind and sincere compliment felt like an eternity. I could feel the emotion brewing in my gut and slowly rising to my chest. It seemed as if Kerri, Chad, and their guests were patiently waiting for my reply. I had to make a decision and quickly. I could give in to the negative emotions of not feeling worthy and let them consume me, as I had become accustomed to doing, or I could embrace and accept that it was OK to feel this and allow the emotions to simply pass through me.

Standing next to my bike, with my head down, I took a deep breath, sheepishly lifted my head, and looked Kerri in her eyes. "Thank you," I said, still not feeling worthy of her compliment. It took everything in me to pull that off, but I did. I then told everyone I needed to move on so I didn't get stiff standing around. I hopped on my bike, clicked into my pedals, wove in and out of the handful of young kids that were playing in the road, and rolled out of the cul-de-sac. As soon as I was confident I was out of sight, I stopped pedaling, pulled over on the side of the road and said out loud, "What the fuck just happened?"

After the incident, I experienced no emotional suffering or increase in physical pain. It's tough to know why. Was it because I was aware of the emotional trigger and dealt with it by acknowledging it, accepting her compliment, and moving on? Or was it because I opted to keep riding my bike, and the physical exercise created harmony in both my body and mind?

I still had many questions, but at least I had some answers.

CHAPTER 17

Placebo, Yoga, and More

While I was making progress, it was subtle. The harder I looked for improvement in my body, the more I became aware of any pain or lingering sensations. It was nearly impossible to observe a light, lingering sensation in my body and feel as if I was making progress. Even if those sensations were indications of improvement.

Signs of healing were coming in quiet ways. First there was my experience riding the tram at Jackson Hole Resort, then there was a sense of calm while reading at home, even while experiencing pain. And as summer rolled on, in addition to feeling more relaxed and stepping up my activity level, other signs of healing were surfacing.

For example, the view from our kitchen's bank of windows looks eastward, out to our beautiful green grass and eight-foot-tall hedges that are shaped like a rolling wave, separating us from the Atlantic Ocean. When we originally looked at the property, I remember standing in the kitchen looking out the windows and feeling as if the house was bobbing in the water, because the hedges created an illusion as if we were actually floating. I had that sensation a handful of times when we first moved in. But now, twelve years later, I was having it again. Just bobbing in the water of life. I also began to notice that our gardens had better colors and longer blooms. Everything seemed just a bit richer.

Then one midsummer day, home by myself, I became aware that I was happy. And for the first time in over two and a half years, I realized how happy I was to be retired. There were certainly times in the past year when I was feeling good, but this was different. I was not in Wyoming fly-fishing in remote creeks or skiing in the backcountry. Nor was I on my road bike, cruising the country roads of New Hampshire. I was lying on the couch, by myself, in the middle of the day, doing nothing. With a smile on my face, I decided to enjoy the peace and empty space that surrounded me and take a nap, guilt free!

The more I witnessed firsthand how the mind can affect the body, the more I thought about other physical issues I'd had over the years. I thought back to my shoulder problems and how the pain had suddenly appeared.

That summer of 2010, I saw two doctors and they provided me no surgical option; they only offered PT and more cortisone shots. This forced me to give up tennis, surfing, and cycling. I could not do anything. A short time later I connected with a doctor in Utah. After a couple of phone conversations discussing my shoulders, I flew out there for the procedure. Yeah, I was committed to surgery prior to him even seeing me or my images. I was excited to hear he could fix me and do it fast. I had a physical exam the day I landed. Then he reviewed the images I had brought. And after signing all the paperwork, I was scheduled for surgery and operated on the following morning. Three months later, I had the same procedure done on my right shoulder. I considered both surgeries to be a success, as they got me back in the game.

But now, since learning about the mind-body connection, I

looked back at the sequence of events with a different perspective. And here's what I now saw: I'd met two doctors and dismissed both quickly, probably because they didn't offer surgery as a solution. Is it possible they didn't suggest surgery because they felt my condition didn't warrant it? And why was the doctor who performed the surgery so confident he could help me without even seeing me or the X-ray?

Is it possible that my shoulder problems were really TMS and a mind-body condition? I mean, the surgery clearly worked. Or maybe it was a placebo effect. A placebo can take any form, from a pill to an injection to a surgical procedure. It's a placebo as long as it does not have any actual therapeutic properties. Any improvement from the placebo is known as the placebo effect. The Food and Drug Administration (FDA) highly regulates any new drug before it hits the market by testing the believed therapeutic effects through the placebo test.

However, the FDA does not require testing on surgical procedures against the placebo effect like it does for drugs. It appears that operations became mainstream based on the perceived benefits. There are certainly ethical questions related to placebo surgeries, such as knowingly exposing a patient to the risk of infection and problems with anesthesia. And then we have the ethics of invasive clinical procedures.

According to Harvard Health Publishing, "The placebo effect is more than positive thinking—believing a treatment or procedure will work. It's about creating a stronger connection between the brain and body and how they work together."[14] I was learning the power of intention and context. It was the act of showing up, and I went with the intention for a desired outcome, believing the doctor

---

14   Harvard Health Publishing, "The Power of the Placebo Effect," August 9, 2019, https://www.health.harvard.edu/mental-health/the-power-of-the-placebo-effect.

could fix me, rather than rolling up my sleeves to do the emotional work that was needed.

In the early 2000s there was a controversial study conducted by a group of doctors led by Dr. Bruce Moseley. He stated, "Many patients report symptomatic relief after undergoing arthroscopy of the knee for osteoarthritis, but it is unclear how the procedure achieves this result. We conducted a randomized, placebo-controlled trial to evaluate the efficacy of the arthroscopy of the knee. A total of 180 patients with osteoarthritis of the knee were randomly assigned to receive arthroscopic debridement, arthroscopic lavage or placebo surgery. Patients in the placebo group received skin incisions and underwent a simulated debridement without insertion of the arthroscope. Patients and assessors of the outcome were blinded to the treatment group assignment. Outcomes were assessed at multiple points over a 24-month period with the use of five self-reported scores—three on scales for pain and two on scales for function—and one objection test of walking and stair climbing. A total of 165 patients completed the trial."[15]

The study concluded that the outcomes after arthroscopic lavage or arthroscopic debridement were not better than those after the placebo procedure.

I was intrigued by this finding. And according to Ian Harris's *Surgery, the Ultimate Placebo*, the author, an orthopedic surgeon, discovered that, "in about half of the fifty-three trials found, surgery was not better than the placebo treatment."[16]

Reading the results of these studies supported my conviction of the powerful role my mind could play on my healing. Placebo or

---

15 Dr. Bruce Moseley, "A Controlled Trial of Arthroscopic Surgery for Osteoarthritis of the Knee," *New England Journal of Medicine*, https://www.nejm.org/doi/full/10.1056/nejmoa013259.

16 Ian Harris, *Surgery, the Ultimate Placebo* (Montgomery, AL: New South, 2016), 83–84.

no placebo, I was grateful I no longer had shoulder pain! While pain was never welcome, I was starting to view the spikes in pain as opportunities for discovery and healing.

While improvement was indeed happening, I noticed more emotional challenges. It was not a constant struggle. More often than not, I felt pretty good. But inevitably something would set me off, and those old emotions would make me feel angry, fearful, or resentful. I found it interesting that as I was seeing improvement in my physical symptoms, my emotional troubles had become more obvious to me.

I shared this with Eric, and he said, "It's very normal to have an increase in emotional suffering, because you're now feeling your emotions, something you probably had never done, and it can be very alarming for those who have been frozen most of their life."

Frozen.

While Eric's comment didn't alleviate my emotional pain, it was always nice to hear what I was experiencing was normal. There would be days that I would feel pretty darn good and think, *If I just did not have this emotional suffering I could live with the physical discomfort.*

It was at that point when I really understood that my emotional pain was there for a purpose. It was just another way my body was talking to me, telling me my healing was not complete, that something was wrong and still out of balance. Now that the proverbial cat was out of the bag, there was no turning back. I was on high alert, ready to notice whatever emotions surfaced.

Early on, while working with Eric, he encouraged me to stay calm when I was triggered. But at the same time, he said with a smile, "I know you will not be able to do that at first, no matter how many times I tell you."

He could not have been more right. Each spike in pain was always accompanied by some sort of fear or anger, which were real emotional struggles for me. It was so hard to determine what was causing what. The pain and burning sensations in my lower legs were constantly moving around. One moment I might feel them at the top of my feet, and a few minutes later it could be on my knees, shins, or the soles of my feet. The movement was like a ghost. As hard as I tried, I could never observe the pain move from one site to the next.

But I also began seeing the sensations in my body differently. I became less fearful of them and formed a sense of attachment to them, like a bond was being created. It was something I had never experienced before. I didn't feel as threatened by the discomfort. But, when the sensations crossed that threshold and became pain, the relationship turned confrontational.

In spite of my challenges, I continued with my meditation practice each day and was doing my own morning yoga session by myself. I would start each day lying on the floor for forty minutes doing a number of different restorative yoga poses while listening to soft, soothing music. Becky had been encouraging me to go to yoga with her, but I just couldn't do it. New situations and people could be intimidating if I perceived them to be outside my wheelhouse. The odd thing about my resistance was, deep down I knew it was something I would enjoy if I could just find the courage to go. I've always been that way, however.

Becky had recently started teaching yoga, in fact, which was a big reason I felt guilty about not going to a class. But so far that guilt hadn't seemed to manifest itself in physical pain. One day, Becky and a few of her fellow teachers organized a yoga and meditation class at a historical garden that would benefit a local yoga and cancer organization. Since the garden was less than a mile away, Becky offered to host a reception after the class at our house. This was the second year for the event, and she was excited leading up to it. I did not go the prior year, as I was a mess emotionally and didn't want to be around people.

Now should have been my chance to make up for it, to make it up to Becky. Besides, I had made significant improvement from the previous year. And I was dialed in to my healing. One may think a yoga–meditation class in a beautiful garden by the ocean would be healing, and you would be right. But as much as I wanted to participate for my wife, I still resisted. Doing yoga with other people and then making small talk with forty yogis at our house afterward made my anxiety skyrocket. Part of me wanted to go, because I knew how important it was to Becky, and I wanted to support her. She'd comforted and encouraged me so much during my difficult journey. But I had this thick, stubborn wall of resistance in front of me, holding me back. Something was saying, "No, don't go!"

Three days before the event I still was undecided. Then a moment came while I was on my road bike listening to an audiobook podcast by Dr. Peter Levine. Dr. Levine studies trauma, its causes, effects, and healing. He is the author of many books, including one that was slowly becoming my favorite: *Waking the Tiger and Healing Trauma.* As I grinded away on my bike, I was drawn to what Dr. Levine was saying:

"Today it is understood that trauma is a common occurrence that can be caused by seemingly benign events. The good news is that we don't have to live with it—at least, not forever. Trauma can be healed and even more easily prevented. Its most bizarre symptoms can be resolved if we are willing to let our natural, biological instincts guide us. To accomplish this, we need to learn a whole new way of understanding and experiencing ourselves. For most of us it's going to be like living in a strange new land."[17]

At that moment, I realized that my healing journey had begun when I trusted my instincts. I knew as soon as I picked up Dr. Sarno's *Healing Back Pain* that the mind-body connection was the path I needed to take—there simply was no question in my mind. No

---

17 Peter A. Levine, *Waking the Tiger: Healing Trauma* (Berkeley, CA: North Atlantic Books, 1997), ch. 4.

more doctors, X-rays, or injections. I did not care what the early naysayers close to me said about my beliefs and conclusions. I was trusting my own instincts. While on my bike, I let go of the resistance and my insecurities and decided to go to the yoga class and the reception.

On the day of the event, it had been threatening rain, but it held off. It was a warm, humid evening with calm winds and an occasional blue sky peeking through the clouds. Jaimie, Kaylee, and I were the first to arrive. The garden was small with lush, green grass, tall, manicured hedges on each side, and three small Roman statues in front with a babbling fountain in the rear. We laid our mats by the fountain, Jaimie on one side of me, Kaylee on the other. I felt safe and secure. As the yogis started to roll in, everyone was incredibly friendly. Some people meditated, some stretched, while others talked quietly. I did it all. Becky began the class, her posture perfect and her voice soft. Between poses, I kept sneaking looks at my caring wife. *How did I get so lucky?*

The whole evening turned out to be an amazing experience. I was so proud of Becky and what she was doing to help others by sharing and guiding a yoga practice. It felt great to support her and one of her passions. We have always had a strong relationship and do a lot of things together, but I was slowly learning how to be more consistent with my support when I was not feeling well. I think about how much energy I spent debating if I would go or not. The wall that I thought was holding me back turned out to be paper-thin. I didn't quite understand why the evening was so powerful, but I now see it is the power of yoga, to be able to let go of something we are not even aware we are holding on to.

A couple of days after Becky's yoga event, I felt OK until I needed to take Kaylee to the airport and couldn't find my wallet. In that moment, not only was my equilibrium lost, but my pain spiked as well. Immediately my feet and lower legs hurt. After dropping

Kaylee off and returning home, I became increasingly frustrated and angry about my lost wallet (the trigger), which caused my pain to spike.

I watched myself getting sucked back into the pain vortex: My mood got sour, and I became quiet. I was in a dark place and could not find peace. I began looking for things to annoy me, simple things. So instead of trying to find a way out, I was feeding the beast. At that moment, I realized this behavior was a chronic pattern.

Often, I would lose control and take it out on Becky. Like, if she was slow getting ready to meet friends for dinner, I'd get in the car and start to stew, starting the evening off on the wrong foot. Or if we got lost going to one of the kids' athletic games, I'd silently blame her, letting the kettle boil, since she was responsible for the directions.

Still unable to effectively regulate those situations, I would step out of the present moment and anger would settle in. Looking back, Becky had amazing patience with me—that of a saint! But saints have their breaking point, too. And when she would reach that point and defend herself, I would declare the argument over, then stew on my own in silence.

But this day was different. I had gained enough awareness through my journey to not take it out on Becky, thank God. But all that meant was less expression or release, as I continued to feed the beast that afternoon. Weeds growing on our walkway, lousy weather in the forecast, or dogs barking to come in right after I let them out, all caused the anger to come in, while nothing went out.

I knew talking to Becky might help, but I just couldn't open up.

Over the course of two days, Becky knew something was wrong, but she gave me my space. She had no idea the degree to which I was suffering, but how could she?

Thirty-six hours after losing my wallet, it finally showed up . . . in Colorado. Ha! It inadvertently got knocked off a shelf into Kaylee's luggage and headed back to school with her. While the news of the wallet helped somewhat, it did not completely free me as I'd hoped. I was still struggling and it was, ironically, made worse by my awareness of my suffering. It was hard for me to navigate life's triggers.

I knew I needed to do something, and finding the wallet gave me just enough drive to start moving. I grabbed my tree saw and pruning equipment and spent the next three hours trimming our 150-year-old linden tree. I've always loved trimming trees and have a good eye for what needs to be removed. I finished up around seven o'clock that evening. With a few hours of daylight remaining, I spent the time by myself sitting in a lawn chair looking at maps of Wyoming while Becky sat in the kitchen.

Every twenty minutes or so I would get up and walk into the kitchen to grab a snack or something to drink and then return to the lawn chair and become absorbed in the maps. On my third trip to the kitchen, I looked at Becky as I entered the room and noticed how she appeared so peaceful curled up in a chair reading. I was so thankful for her support, love, and her giving me my space. At that very moment, I felt something happening inside of me. It was sudden, but I was able to witness it. I felt as if someone removed a drain plug from the side of my head and all the negative, shitty feelings were pouring out of me. By the time I got a handful of pretzels at the far end of the kitchen, I realized I was free. And just like that, all the emotional suffering was gone. The experience was so clear, there was no need for me to *think* about what had just happened. I knew at some point I would break free, but this was the first time I was able to witness that kind of experience.

Why did the anguish leave me at that moment? Was it the physical activity of trimming a tree? Or was it sitting by myself looking at maps, both of which I love to do? Maybe it was my observation of Becky so peaceful in the kitchen? Or maybe it was not that complicated, and it was just time for me to let go and let it out.

That night, I thought about the week and the roller-coaster ride it had been. I wanted to share all of that with Becky. Plus, I felt it was important to my own healing to talk to her about my inability at times to open up when I am struggling. The next morning, as the early sun rose and filled our kitchen with light and warmth, I took a deep breath, feeling very unsure of myself, and said, "I was really struggling the past few days." I was relieved I was able to share those few words with her. However, that relief did not last long, and Becky simply said, "Yeah, I knew you weren't yourself."

And then I was triggered. I suddenly felt the need to protect myself. Instantaneously, I recoiled and shut down and told her I didn't want to talk about it. There is not much that gets by me these days, so I was completely aware of what I'd just done. But it happened so quickly I knew it was not a conscious decision.

Stop! Danger. Do not proceed. The message my subconscious had sent me effectively shut down a conversation that could have been very healing for both of us. I couldn't understand why I had been triggered by such a simple remark. Ironically, what could have pulled us closer in that moment triggered me to pull away. I thought, if I could just understand what my subconscious was trying to protect me from, I would be on the path to greater peace.

CHAPTER 18

Trauma and My Dad

From the time I discovered Dr. Sarno and TMS, I was committed to learning as much as I could. Good or bad, right or wrong, I needed to understand. My healing trajectory went from learning about TMS and the mind-body connection to getting in touch with the broader scope of suffering and trauma.

In addition to all the reading I was doing, I was learning more about my father's childhood, which was difficult to process. I never understood the degree to which he had suffered. Neither he nor my mother spoke about it all that much. Recently, in an effort to help me with my healing, my mother shared poignant stories about my father with me. Some I knew about, others I did not. When my father was twelve years old, he was smoking cigarettes and playing with matches when his pants caught on fire. A neighbor next door happened to be outside at the time, beating a rug, and saw my father on fire and ran over with the rug and rolled my father up into it, putting the fire out and saving his life.

My father had been badly burned on one leg. He had multiple

operations and spent a year in the hospital. After he was released, he had some anger problems and was getting into trouble at school. His father ended up sending him to what my father referred to as "bad boys" school for two years. After his time at reform school, and as he got a bit older, his mother became ill. Soon after, his parents determined he was too much to handle and sent him to live with his aunt for a couple of years, a few hours away. Between the ages of eleven and eighteen, five of those eight years were spent living away from his family.

But he was a survivor and ended up going to Northeastern University in Boston to play football. Unfortunately, that lasted only six months, as my father was kicked off the team because he got into a heated argument with the coach. Learning this about my father taught me this: The effects of childhood trauma will carry over into adulthood.

My father was simply unable to control his emotions at times. And I am convinced it started when he was young. I thought back to a passage in a book I'd read by Dr. Nadine Burke Harris, *The Deepest Well: Healing the Long-Term Effects of Childhood Adversity*:

> Twenty years of medical research has shown that childhood adversity literally gets under our skin, changing people in ways that can endure in their bodies for decades. It can tip a child's developmental trajectory and affect physiology. It can trigger chronic inflammation and hormonal changes that can last a lifetime. It can alter the way DNA is read and how cells replicate, and it can dramatically increase the risk for heart disease, stroke, cancer, diabetes—even Alzheimer's.[18]

I wondered what it must have been like for him to spend a year in the hospital. Why did he need to be there for an entire year? And

---

18 Nadine Burke Harris, *The Deepest Well: Healing the Long-Term Effects of Childhood Adversity* (Boston: Mariner Books, 2018), XV.

once he was released from the hospital, how did he feel when he was sent away for two years to reform school? Did he make friends? Did his father visit him? What was going through my father's mind once he returned and his father told him his mother was ill and he needed to go live with his aunt?

The person who endured all this was not the six-foot-three, 250-pound man that I knew. He was just a kid.

I was simultaneously saddened and curious to learn this and I wondered what effect these experiences had on him. How did his past make him the man and father I knew?

What emotions did he have as a child? Anger, resentment, fear? What behaviors might he have developed to protect himself?

One afternoon, an article online caught my attention. California had recently named its first surgeon general, and one of the stated goals for this newly minted doctor was to screen every student for adverse childhood experiences (ACEs). And, as I continued reading, I discovered the new appointee was the same Dr. Nadine Burke Harris!

The article gave an example: "Before entering school, the school nurse would get a note from a physician that says, 'Here is the care plan for this child's toxic stress. And this is how it shows up.' The use of detention, suspension, or expulsion produces greater negative effects; and rather than saying to a child, 'What's wrong with you?' we will ask, 'What happened to you?'"

She then added, "Trauma in general leads to a surge in stress hormones. When this trauma goes unchecked and is sustained, it can disrupt a child's brain development, interfering with functions children depend on in school such as memory recall, focus, and impulse control."[19]

---

19   Patrice Gaines and Esta Pratt-Kielley, "California's first surgeon general: Screen every student for childhood trauma," NBC News, October 11, 2019, https://www.nbcnews.com/news/nbcblk/california-s-first-surgeon-general-screen-every-student-childhood-trauma-n1064286.

After reading that article, I was certain my father had never been asked the question "What happened to you?" when he was young. He'd probably blamed himself. That's how it works; kids blame themselves. It's what I did, too. Kids and their developing brains need safe, stable environments. It would be hard to imagine how he could have had that growing up.

+   +   +

As time went on, I found being triggered had its own flow, its own mini-cycle. First, I felt a subtle shift in my body. Next, there would be emotional struggles (anger, fear, etc.) and then physical pain. My reaction at this point would be to isolate myself and then do some sort of inquiry, often during meditation, that would typically lead to inner discovery, and ultimately, release of pain.

One such cycle triggered another increase in groin pain, but I made sure to keep up with my meditation practice, switching from guided meditation to silent meditation: I also continued to read. When I first started meditating, I knew nothing about the origins of meditation, I just did it. And it seemed to be working.

Recently I learned that Buddhism has its roots in *mindfulness*, the practice of learning to be happy and aware in the present moment. Mindfulness is a stable happiness, a happiness we can rely on, because it contains calmness and contentment. It is reliable because it depends on our own intention, not conditions and circumstances. That is what I had experienced when I had a sense of peace and calmness, yet I was still in pain. The Buddha also taught about "impermanence," which is the reality that all things are changing, including our moods, the weather, our thoughts, relationships, and even us! The problem is that we cling to things as if they are permanent or we resist the reality of what is. The Buddha said, "When we understand that all things are impermanent, we can begin to find meaning and joy in every moment as it passes."

While I didn't know any of this when I started, I could relate to what Buddha was teaching. He speaks of different kinds of happiness like going on vacation, receiving an award, or having a satisfying meal (and even skiing powder). These are all good, but the feelings associated with them are temporary.

Yes, yes, yes, that made total sense to me! I was resisting reality and the experience of what is. I needed to let go. I needed to let go of the fear or the unknown of what would happen with the groin pain. Or any pain.

I seemed to be able to let go at times. But as I looked closer at those times, it became clear they were the moments when I was pain free. *Shit.* It was the fear or clinging that had prevented me from being present. And I had been learning through reading and life experiences, if I am not present, then I'm missing all the subtleties of life.

My preoccupation with the latest groin pain, for example, was doing me no good. I wasn't figuring anything out, not solving a problem. Damn it, I wasn't even sure if there *was* a problem. I could do all my activities with a bit of discomfort during idle times. All I was doing was creating tension in my body with my fear. They say in Buddhism that denial of reality ends up hurting us. And I couldn't agree more.

What the Buddha taught about mindfulness, impermanence, and clinging did not free me from my suffering, but it made sense, gave me hope, and showed me *the way*. Still trying to process the spike in groin pain, I had my scheduled call with Eric. I told him about the groin pain and fear of my hip failing me, the increase in pain in my lower legs, and just how disappointed I felt about everything. I continued to ramble on. I told him that I wasn't trying to offend him, but after ten months of therapy, I asked him where it had gotten me. Then, not waiting for a response from Eric, pissed off and in pain, I asked, "What have I actually accomplished here, Eric?"

With a quick breath, I answered my own question: "I've gained more confidence in my ability to exercise. I am aware that my body speaks to me. I can see and feel my emotional triggers. My anxiety is way down, and I am much more patient."

Not fully aware of what I had rattled off, I finished with two more questions: "So, I ask you, Eric, is that healing? Do I have too many emotional layers of trauma to be able to heal?"

Exhausted from this impromptu assault on my therapist, I became silent and just waited for Eric to respond. "Thank you for feeling comfortable enough to share how you are feeling, Mike. I am sorry to hear that you are still in pain. Have you discussed this with Becky?"

Irritated that he'd glossed over the pain portion and sandwiched it in with a question about my wife, I offered little in response: "No."

There was a pause and then Eric said, "I see. I thought you would have shared these feelings with her. Is there a reason you have chosen not to tell Becky?"

I thought for a moment and honestly, I didn't know why I hadn't opened up to Becky yet. That wall was there again. It was hard for me to be open when I was hurting. The wall that was preventing me from sharing was real. But the conversation with Eric gave me just enough clarity to be able to remove that wall and tell Becky about the increase in pain I'd been experiencing.

The next day, as Becky and I sat on the front steps of the house, I said, "I'm just so tired of having setbacks. Whenever I make some headway, the pain sets in, sometimes even worse, and I'm swept back again. And now this groin pain. I was hoping to hike tomorrow, but now I don't know what to do."

"Just go!" Becky said. "The mountains always make you feel better. And even if the pain doesn't subside, your mind will feel better. You have made so much progress, keep following your instinct. You'll be fine, plus the White Mountains will be absolutely gorgeous tomorrow!"

I grinned and went to grab my maps. I had a hike to plan!

At seven o'clock the next morning I was at the trailhead in Crawford Notch. I was going to challenge myself by hiking New Hampshire's southern Presidential Range. It was a hike I'd never done, over nine miles and five thousand feet of climbing. Most of the hike was above the tree line, capturing five of the forty-eight peaks in New Hampshire that are over four thousand feet in elevation—Mounts Jackson, Pierce, Eisenhower, and Monroe and finishing at the summit of Mount Washington. It was a perfect New England fall day. Plenty of blue sky and summit temperatures in the mid-50s. When I reached the first peak, Mount Jackson, the pain in my lower legs had all but dissolved, and while my left groin felt tight at times, there was never an *ouch* moment the entire day. I finished the hike in just under six hours. It was a great day to be in the mountains, touching nature from high above the valley floor.

The hike was the beginning of my ability to let go. Let go of the tightness, the pain, the worry, everything. The hike helped me push forward in all areas of my life. I became more comfortable with the tightness in the groin that would present itself at times. And the best part is, I was no longer as focused on the pain as I had been. I was starting to see another way through it. I began to see that by taking the focus off the pain and engaging in an activity that I enjoyed such as hiking, without worrying whether I could do the hike or if the pain would return, I experienced the first taste of freedom from pain's hold over me for the past two years. There was also tremendous growth coming out of every triggered event, realizing I held the answers by listening to my pain-body. It was also empowering, after the pain subsided, to realize that I was not broken and that healing could happen. I was also experiencing the positive effects communicating had on me, whether that was with Eric, Dr. Stracks, or Becky.

This newfound energy and perspective from the hike allowed me to move forward with my healing and inspired me to develop a yoga practice—one that would, over time, play a critical role in easing my suffering and pain. I also began to join Becky at the yoga studio where she taught. It was not clear to me at first why I became committed to yoga and what the actual draw was, but after a week or so of going to yoga, I looked forward to going each day and always walked out of class feeling better than when I walked in. Always.

While the yoga was improving my flexibility, balance, and strength, after practicing daily for a few weeks in a row, its real pull was the emotional and spiritual lift I was experiencing during and after each class. The simple act of practicing yoga seemed to be opening me up to greater awareness. In fact, after each yoga session, my willingness to be open and communicate was shocking in itself. It surprised me and would take me a minute or two after I walked out of class to embrace those feelings. This way of communicating was foreign to me.

One evening after yoga, I decided to do an evening meditation. Feeling very relaxed from my yoga session and with the lights on, I lay down and was immediately overcome by powerful emotions. I felt lonely, sad, and very scared. It felt like a switch had been thrown as the emotions appeared out of the blue. This startled me, but at the same time, for whatever reason, I did not run from it, nor did I open my eyes. Something also prevented me from moving. In spite of the discomfort, I became unconsciously curious. I felt as if I could see and feel my emotions! Lonely, sad, and scared were right in front of me. But they did not hurt.

How could that be? I felt removed from the whole situation. Yet, I knew I was still experiencing my emotions. But they were not controlling me. In that moment, there was no pain. I was simply witnessing my own emotions. To feel and see my own fear and sadness, but to be removed from it so it did not hurt, was just incredible!

As the experience played out, I was unsure what was happening and perhaps a bit nervous that the emotions would consume me and I would start to feel them in a deep way. I slowly got up and, as I walked downstairs, I thought I was in a fog, only to realize it was the complete opposite. I had the most amazing clarity I'd ever experienced in my entire life. Everything was perfectly clear. There was zero distortion as I continued to witness my emotions. By the time I got to the kitchen, the experience was gone. I had many questions about what happened but had a sense that my meditation and yoga practices were bringing me to something very profound.

PART 3:

Awakening Emotions and Purpose

CHAPTER 19

Early Retirement

As my understanding of trauma and the role prolonged periods of stress have on the body, I found myself revisiting past periods of my life with a different perspective. Though most of my physical problems happened almost ten years after I retired, as I continued on the healing path, I realized the stress I was under while working was much greater than I had wanted to believe. And even more important was how I chose to deal with that stress, or in my case, not deal with it.

In the summer of 1993, when I was twenty-nine years old, my older brother David developed a business plan based on a unique direct marketing strategy. With seed money from my brother-in-law, Chris, they started a business in the finance industry and asked me to be part of the company. My brother and brother-in-law had both been very successful in their business careers. I had always respected them and jumped at the opportunity to team up. From day one, it was clear we were on to something special, and their vision to sell the company in the future was plausible, based on the early success. I was blessed to have three very smart business partners, with Jim, Chris's younger brother, being the third. All three had great, forward-thinking vision, seeing angles most could not.

In less than two years we had more than two dozen employees while still growing at a rapid pace. With the early success and the continued growth, conflict arose among the four partners. It quickly escalated and became confrontational. After months of significant tension, less than three years after we started the business, Jim, Chris, and I bought out my brother—the very business he founded. During that time, our disagreement, conflict, and ultimate separation swept through our family like a raging wildfire. Sides were taken, and my parents became emotionally involved. Tensions were extremely high; from 1996 to 1999 it was difficult for everyone involved. I dealt with the stress by ignoring the family dynamics that were in play and—per usual, my emotions—completely committing myself to my work. It was the only way I knew how to deal with it.

Once my brother left, Jim and I were responsible for the day-to-day operations. Jim focused on technology and marketing, and I handled the growing sales team. I had a bit of a reputation of being the ballbuster, and I guess I embraced that. I was a man of few words, yet was always very direct with people, speaking with truth and honesty. I was completely committed to the process of helping the sales representatives succeed and took great pride in achieving that. One of the proudest days for Jim and me was when one of our early employees was able to purchase his first house because our company provided him with the financial stability to do so. At times, I could step back and take pride in what I'd accomplished. But accepting a compliment from someone else, like Kerri in the cul-de-sac, was a different matter altogether,

It was a fast-paced environment and there was seldom time to reflect on our success. Like a lot of business owners, I imagine, I always operated out of fear of failure. The insecurities I had about my worth were ever-present while helping to run the company. It's the reason I worked so hard.

I recently found a letter from Jim wishing me a happy birthday. This was written after eleven years in business together and three years before the sale of a portion of our company to a venture capital (VC) firm. At this point, we had been through so much. We were both thrust into the leadership roles when my brother left. Not only did we survive, we also thrived and developed a cohesive working partnership. And while we had success early and often, there were pivotal moments that required significant teamwork between the two of us and quick decision-making to keep the company in business. With the turnover in our sales management team, the effects the dot-com bust had on our business, and having to reinvent our approach to generating sales leads, it often felt as if it was Jim and me against the world.

This is the letter Jim sent me on my fortieth birthday:

You are the man, Mike. I can't believe you hit the big 4-0! You're a role model for drive and youth, bro!

It's rare two guys come into a start-up business the way we did. It's even rarer for two guys to be such an awesome team. I wanted to take this moment to tell you how pumped I am to be your partner. I don't think there is a better two-punch team than you and I. Your drive, passion, and compassion for our people create the fuel that makes them jam and deliver our service so well. You are a master of many trades and making people better is on top of the list. The respect I and they have for you is tremendous. Our roots go deep. We've been through so much and have driven through it only by sticking together and by never giving up. As the cliche goes, "That which doesn't destroy you, makes you stronger." I truly feel we have lived this in business and in our relationship and is something I enjoy in a deep way. I know you rarely or ever kick back and relish who and what you are, so I want to say thank you for being you and for being in business with me.

Here's to where we are able to go. The sweetness of working to achieve wealth with our many one step back and two forward is the concrete that makes this company so damn good.

Cheers MJM!

Jim

It's funny what happens when you clean the lens through which you see life unfold. I remember receiving this letter, feeling good about it, proud for a moment, only to quickly put it away. The more I tried to allow his kind words to fill me with a sense of accomplishment, the stronger the desire was to forget the words of appreciation.

In 2006, we were approached by a VC firm, and they made an overture to buy a stake in our company. The initial valuation offered was significant. For the next ten months, our partner Chris negotiated with the VC firm while Jim and I continued to run the business. It was an exciting time. To dream about having a liquidity event that would provide me with enough wealth to retire if I wanted to was exciting. During this time, I began to wonder what life would be like with our new partner. I'd had such autonomy the past thirteen years, I was unsure what the next phase would look like for me.

In March 2007, the deal funded and I became a very wealthy man. Unsurprisingly, this pile of cash I was now sitting on did little to alleviate my anxiety, an emotion that was never obvious to the outside observer, but was often there, simmering just below the surface. In fact, the money probably made it worse in some ways. At times, because of my newfound wealth, I felt as if I did not meet the standards of someone in my position. With a new partner in the VC firm, there were more meetings and more goals being set. I just wanted to work as hard as I could and help those who worked for me become successful. I realized it was hardly a sophisticated corporate philosophy. But now I see it is what made a great, successful team.

Unfortunately, I was not comfortable with the situation. Our new partners were well educated and very successful investment bankers. When they visited our office to do their due diligence on our company, the two areas they were most interested in seeing (and impressed with) were our technology (Jim's responsibility) and the organization of our sales floor (my responsibility). Our sales floor was stuffed with energy and covered with dozens of talented, fun, hard-charging people. The sales floor was our secret weapon and it showed incredibly well.

It was tough not to feed off that environment. But I did not think it was quite enough—or I was not quite enough—and I would be exposed over time. I was experiencing Imposter Syndrome, which is a form of intellectual self-doubt. It's when achievers are unable to internalize their success. They falsely believe they are not as competent as others see them to be. I was on edge, unhappy, and kept all my concerns to myself. Four months after the VC company purchased shares in our business, I notified my two partners of my decision to leave. While there were mixed emotions, I felt tremendous relief once I spoke with each of them.

As I fully expected, redeeming my remaining stock shares in the company was not a simple or painless process. It was complicated, as part of the original sale had future earn-outs with benchmarks set. Valuing those future dollars to current dollars proved challenging. I was now at odds with the VC company as well as my two business partners of thirteen years. It was a painful process with many heated arguments over valuation and my remaining payout.

I was advised as we negotiated not to tell anyone of my situation and decision. I found myself living in limbo. It was as if I had disappeared. I communicated with no one and did not return the calls from the sales reps who I had a strong bond with and were wondering where I was. I even was forced to keep this from our kids until a decision on value had been agreed upon. Instead of being at the office all day, I stayed at home. After 108 days following my absence from the office, the transaction was completed, and I was no longer an employee or a stockholder.

Looking back at my days of working, it's unfortunate that I did not fully recognize and accept my talents. I was so focused on what I believed I did not know. But even that proved to be mostly a mirage, driven by the patterns of the past. I failed to consistently embrace that having a successful partnership, which we had, was a special gift, that the beauty of it was just that—it was a partnership and we each bring our own unique talents to the table.

As I reflected on this period and how I chose to once again close myself off to my emotions, I can see signs of problems with my mind-body connection that I ignored. How I chose to deal with stress was affecting me in ways I was unable to see at the time. A few years before joining my brother and brother-in-law in business, I had become a dedicated tennis player every spring, summer, and fall. I played three to four times per week.

I was self-taught, so my strokes had some flaws, particularly my backhand. My forehand was my weapon. It was consistent, had a lot of topspin, and I became pretty effective at running around my backhand to hit my forehand. After playing tennis regularly for seven years, I developed problems with my tennis game. My forehand disappeared. I would be unable to get my arm, hand, and racket to do what they should. This was not a case of having an off day or driving the ball just outside the lines. This was very different. My forehand stroke felt disconnected, almost foreign. I couldn't understand what was happening. I shared this with a number of people and they openly laughed and had no idea what I was talking about. I was forced to give up tennis, a game I was passionate about. I knew there was an issue, that what was happening to my body was not normal, but I had no idea what it was.

During this time I just couldn't get my body to do what my mind wanted and what I had done successfully for so many years. These were some of the first signs of disharmony between my mind-body, a disconnection that would ultimately push me into chronic pain. I called myself a tennis player, so I was riddled with anxiety and frustration dealing with this problem. Tennis provided me with such joy. I loved the competition and the camaraderie, but I found myself simply incapable of hitting my forehand—my best stroke. Once I could no longer deal with the frustration and embarrassment, I quit tennis cold turkey.

That's probably why years later, I fought so hard to hold on to skiing and hiking when my body started to betray me. I simply couldn't give up my other passions. Even for someone who was still frozen, I knew how painful that loss could be.

CHAPTER 20

Kripalu

I n October of 2019, I attended a three-day seminar at the Kripalu Center in the Berkshires of Massachusetts. Kripalu is a yoga and meditation retreat center, devoted to holistic healing and personal transformation. This was way, *way* outside my comfort zone, and I even surprised myself when I decided to go. I was excited and nervous at the same time. While I had fully embraced yoga and meditation, I had specifically chosen to go to Kripalu to attend a program conducted by Dr. Peter Levine. He was the leader in the field of stress and trauma, the author of *Waking the Tiger,* and the founder of Somatic Experiencing˚.

At the conference, I gained a greater understanding of trauma and learned that it happens when our natural defensive responses become overwhelmed. It's like an injury to our autonomic nervous system that affects our ability to self-regulate. When we feel our lives are threatened, our bodies naturally charge up for fight or flight. If neither of those two options are available, we fall back to the third option, one I had no idea existed—*freeze mode*. This is designed to trick a predator into thinking we're dead, such as a possum, giving us an opportunity to escape later. However, in trauma, we stay stuck in the freeze phase and cannot process the experience. The energy that could have been discharged via fight or flight is instead absorbed into the nervous system because we are frozen.

I'd been playing possum my whole life!

At the retreat I learned that accumulated stress over long periods of time can push the nervous system into collapse and can lead to a variety of conditions that are difficult to diagnose, including chronic pain, fatigue, fibromyalgia, autoimmune disorders, plantar fasciitis, panic attacks, anxiety, alcohol and drug abuse, emotional struggles, and so much more.

I discovered that trauma was not about the upsetting event itself but was the biological and physiological response to that event. Trauma is the energy that gets locked in our body, regardless of whether the event is real or perceived. Trauma hinders the nervous system's ability to maintain a state of balance and pushes you back into fight, flight, or freeze. As Dr. Levine explained, "A traumatized person's nervous system is not damaged; it is frozen in a kind of suspended animation."

Dr. Levine developed Somatic Experiencing to help heal trauma. He believes healing comes from experiencing the physical body and sensations. He studied animals in the wild and observed how they dealt with a traumatic event, such as fleeing from a predator. He explained that once the animal is safe from danger, they are seen shaking and trembling. He says that shaking is instinctual behavior and the animal's way of discharging all of the fight, flight, or freeze energy.

However, we don't need to be chased by a saber-toothed tiger to be forced into the freeze–immobility phase. It can happen any time our natural defense mechanisms become overwhelmed, whether that threat is real or perceived. Regardless, we need to be able to release that energy to maintain a healthy nervous system. Somatic Experiencing helps with trauma by completing the self-protective responses, by releasing that survival energy that is still bound in the body.

One of the main reasons I had some apprehension attending the seminar is because I figured there would be breakout sessions—something I despised. But this new version of me was becoming more open to new experiences and the draw to Somatic Experiencing was far greater than the anxiety of having to talk to strangers.

At the first lecture, I sat at the far end of the front row. The large, sunlit room had a stage at the front and many rows of seats. Approximately fifty participants filled the old conference hall. At some point, Dr. Levine asked each of us to stand up and walk around the hall, to feel the sensations on each foot as it landed on the floor. He then instructed us to keep moving, but to make eye contact with others as we passed them. Dr. Levine would say things like: What are you feeling? Do you feel anything different in the body? Does your face feel warm? Notice any change in your body.

My face did not feel any different, but I could feel my anxiety increase as I made eye contact and moved on. My hands were becoming sweaty, but I was doing OK as long as I kept moving. Dr. Levine then told us to stop and make eye contact with someone and to hold that eye contact for five minutes.

My anxiety skyrocketed. If I could have run and hid, I would have. As I looked for a willing partner, I felt the moisture pooling in my hands and large beads of sweat running down the length of both sides of my spine. The drops of sweat became very cool as they continued down my lower body. I finally locked eyes with a middle-aged woman. I was charged with energy and wanted to break off eye contact, but I held on with everything I had. Once the exercise was done, I was drenched in sweat as I took my seat at the end of the front row.

The next lecture that evening, I changed my seat. Instead of the front row, which consisted of yogi-style cushions on the floor, I chose a chair right in the middle of the third row. An hour into the lecture, we were again asked to stand up and slowly walk around. Dr. Levine then told us to partner up with someone for a closed-eye, walking meditation exercise in which we were asked again to pay attention to the physical sensations that arose.

Fear, anxiety, and sweat took over my body again as I searched for a willing partner. Thankfully, I quickly made eye contact with a young woman in her early thirties. We didn't have time for any introduction, as we each took turns walking the other through the hall by gently holding the other's arm, guiding each other through the crowd of other participants who were doing the same.

During meditation that night, I spent some time reflecting on both exercises. In retrospect, my reaction to both seemed excessive. I even considered leaving the retreat, but I couldn't think of a good excuse to tell Becky. For a moment I thought about calling an old friend to see if I could crash at his place to hide out for a couple of days—all to avoid the next breakout session.

Still in meditation, I dismissed that idea and I wondered why my body had reacted like that. I had never seen my body purge that much moisture outside of exercising. It was then I realized my body was talking to me. What was it saying? Obviously I had some great fear. As I went deeper into reflective meditation, I recognized that the interaction I had with each woman was not that difficult or painful. So, what was with all that sweat pouring down each side of my spine?

I continued to follow my thoughts like a bloodhound and soon found myself thinking about the seat I had chosen in the lecture hall: third row, smack dab in the middle. Why there? I hate being in the middle. I'm always on an aisle seat for easy escape, no matter what the venue. Just ask Becky. I then realized that I unconsciously chose that seat to be surrounded by more people. But why? I'm usually uncomfortable around people I don't know. And then it hit me. I knew that we would be asked to partner up with people or to talk in small groups. Being on the end gave me limited options to partner with someone and more likely to be left out and not chosen. I then completed my reflection and understanding of myself. I was not afraid of talking to someone I did know. I was not afraid of having to express myself. I was simply afraid of not being chosen. I was afraid to be left by myself, alone and embarrassed, while everyone else partnered up. While that experience was not the point of the retreat, I think being there in that type of spiritual setting allowed me the security to recognize and accept some of my childhood fears.

Remaining in my meditative state, I was drawn back to third grade when the whole backside of my hand was covered with warts. At the time it seemed like hundreds of them. It was so embarrassing, and I did everything I could to hide them. During PE class, we were being taught how to dance. I wasn't sure what I was more scared of at the time—the girls seeing my wart-covered hand, or not being chosen at all. I remember times like that day in PE very well. Frozen in fear, trying to become invisible, in hopes that no one would see me—a pattern that had now become very familiar. I wasn't sure what this meant for my healing, but it was clear I was getting to know myself on a much deeper level than I ever had before.

CHAPTER 21

Releasing Energy

D r. Levine's Kripalu lecture deepened my understanding of trauma, the role that our fight, flight, or freeze responses play, and how our body stores that energy if it is not released. That stockpiled energy ultimately becomes the lightning rod for future triggers. Releasing that energy and allowing it to pass through you is critical. Understanding that idea allowed me to look more closely at two experiences I had gone through a year prior.

The first was the year earlier, in January 2018, when my good friend Matt encouraged me to meet him in Vermont to ski, as a mid-week storm was heading that way. As I made the three-hour drive from New Hampshire to Vermont that morning, the snow was falling at a pretty good clip. When I got on the interstate, the highway, surprisingly, had not been plowed and there were already four inches of wet snow on the road. With my two corgis as my copilots, we slowly drove north under a reduced posted speed limit of forty-five miles per hour.

In the right lane, I saw a white pickup truck a half mile ahead.

At this point, the highway was straight, going slightly downhill. The white pickup truck moved over to the left lane because of a very slow-moving sedan in front of him. I could tell the sedan was moving sluggishly, but I didn't panic, since it was about a half mile in front of me. *Plenty of time for me to slow down.* I hit my brakes, but because of the wet, slick snow, my SUV, instead of slowing down, sped up. My vehicle was not stopping, nor was I slowing down, and I was quickly closing the gap between me and the sedan in front of me. With my foot still pressed to the floorboards, I was waiting for the brakes to work and gain some sense of control. Unfortunately, that never happened. That's when I realized I was going to hit the sedan. All I could do was brace for impact.

Within seconds I hit the sedan and the collision was violent. The sound of metal on metal is one I will never forget. My airbag deployed and my hood folded up, preventing me from seeing out the front window as I was spun around, ending up in the opposite direction, facing south in the northbound lane. My engine was still running, but smoke was coming out of the hood. Unable to see out my window, I opened my door and maneuvered my vehicle onto the shoulder and stopped about thirty yards behind the car I'd hit. The rear end of the sedan looked like an accordion and was pushed into the backseat. My heart sank. A Good Samaritan was already by the driver's-side door, leaning in.

Before I got too close, I yelled to him, "Is the driver all right?"

With a cell phone in his hand, talking to the police, the man told me, "No, no, she's not all right."

I struggled to catch my breath as I returned to my car in a state of disbelief. My mind was racing. *What if she can't walk again? Worse yet, what if she succumbs to her injuries and dies? Her family will be devastated. Will I go to jail for this? How can I handle jail time emotionally? What about my family and our assets? Will I lose everything I've worked so hard for?*

After the longest twenty minutes of my life, the first responders arrived. One paramedic ran up to the car I'd hit and one stayed with me. He wanted me to sit down but I refused. He asked if my neck hurt or if I had any tingling or strange sensations in my arms and legs. For a moment I found humor in that question, considering my recent track record with pain. I told him, "Nope, no tingling or sensations in my arms or legs here."

Now, standing alone on the side of the road, I sent Becky a text, saying that I was in a bad accident, but I was OK. In seconds, my phone lit up with a call from her. I could not pick up, as the paramedic insisted on taking my vitals. The phone continued to ring and when I finally was able to answer it, she was barely able to control her worry:

"Mike! You weren't answering! Are you OK?"

"I'm fine, but the car is—"

"Oh my gosh. Are you hurt at all? Is anyone else hurt? How are the dogs? What happened? Are you sitting down? Where are you? Should I come and get you?"

"Hon, I'm fine, but I'm not sure about the girl driving the other car. I slammed into her on accident. With all the snow and ice . . . Look, I need to get in touch with Mike. I'll call you back in a bit."

I then sent our financial adviser and good friend Mike a message about the accident, telling him I was also concerned about any potential liability. I felt guilty for even thinking of that, let alone asking the question. But it was one that kept racing through my mind, and I had to get it out, or the worry would have consumed me.

For almost an hour and a half, I stood on the side of the highway under falling wet snow, thinking I may have altered someone's life forever. My anxiety was through the roof. I was very concerned about the other driver, and I also wondered how my body would react to this extreme stress.

They finally walked the woman into the ambulance and based on what I could see, she was not terribly hurt. Hell, she was walking! That evening I received a call from the police, and I was relieved to hear she was just fine with no serious injuries and had been sent home. *Thank God.*

With that main concern out of the way, my thoughts shifted to how my body would react to the stressful day. I spoke with Becky and a couple of friends that evening, sharing details about the accident and decompressing. Unbeknownst to me, these conversations—releasing the powerful emotions I was feeling—allowed the stressful energy I'd accumulated from the accident to pass through me. There was no physical pain or emotional suffering in the hours or days to come. That did not mean I was numb to the event, quite the opposite. I was definitely shaken, but I allowed myself to experience the full cycle of those emotions—start to finish.

Dr. Levine had spoken of this process at the retreat. He said the key to avoiding the effects of trauma is to encourage a return to a balanced nervous system. I believe that by talking about the incident, I allowed the energy to pass through me and was able to release it. Instead of holding on to the emotions and suffering like I had been so accustomed to doing my whole life, I released the trauma, which enabled my body to naturally return to a state of balance.

In a separate incident, about a month later, I experienced something similar. I would learn, by looking back at that day, that difficult emotions do not need to lead to suffering. I would also learn more about myself.

A storm was heading to Wyoming, and I'd booked a flight on two days' notice to chase the snow that should last days. I would fly from Boston to Denver and from there it's a short one-hour flight to Jackson Hole. When I landed in Denver, I checked the weather in Jackson and saw that it was already snowing there, and a winter storm warning had been issued. I started to worry that my flight from Denver would not be able to get into Jackson because of the storm. I knew from experience, once the airport is closed, it generally stays closed for the duration of the storm cycle. In this case, it would be four or five days.

As soon as the flight was canceled, there was a mad dash to the United Airlines customer service counter, where there was a line of almost one hundred people, most of whom were trying to get to Jackson. I felt the anxiety and tension begin to build in my body. I would be stranded in Denver, unable to ski that wonderful, deep Wyoming powder for days to come. Sure, it was a first-world problem, but as I would learn, these struggles really were not about skiing or how deep the snow was; they were about my inability to deal with something outside my control and the emotions that followed as a result. If it was not skiing, or my kids' disappointment, I'm sure something else would set me off. If I held on to those experiences, allowing them to grow stronger and stronger, they would consume me.

I waited for a few minutes, but there was zero movement in the line. My frustration, anger, and impatience continued to rise. I decided to call Avis and reserved a car from Denver to Jackson. I hung up the phone, and as I grabbed my backpack off the floor, a group of four skiers standing in front of me looked at me with part disbelief and part admiration and asked, "You're driving to Jackson now?"

I grinned. "Yup," I said and start running to the exit. This move was a gamble. I was confident flights would not be getting into Jackson anytime soon. But it was also two o'clock in the afternoon. It was a good eight-hour drive from Denver to Jackson, and the storm would be coming from the northwest, so there was a good chance I'd drive right into it.

Time was of the essence. One bad move would ruin the whole plan. With my game face on, I was in the rental car in record time. I had done the drive before. The only problem was that I had no idea how to get to Interstate 25 from Denver International Airport, but I knew it was not far. My rental vehicle had GPS, but I figured that it would take too much time to load the route. Bad decision. Instead, I asked the attendant when I pulled out of the car rental lot for directions.

So much for that plan; he was no help at all. I decided I'd just use the mountain range as a guide, since Highway 25 passes right along the Front Range. However, that plan didn't work either, as the sky had become milky with the impending storm and the Rocky Mountains were obscured. I still didn't pull over and load the GPS, because I told myself surely there must be a sign for the highway coming up soon.

Not only did I not pass a sign, but I appeared to be literally driving in circles. Nothing looked familiar, and everything looked the same. I was ready to explode. Instead of simply pulling over to load the GPS, I kept driving while I tried to call Becky for directions. I had now been driving in circles for forty-five minutes. With each passing moment, I realized I was reducing my chances of getting to Jackson before the storm hit and the highways closed.

Becky finally picked up the phone.

I was short and to the point with her. "I don't know where I am, and I can't find the damn interstate!" She tried to help by first asking me where I was. Unable to think clearly, I struggled to control my emotions that had built up over the past two hours. I lost control.

"Beck, IF I KNEW WHERE I WAS I WOULDN'T BE CALLING YOU!"

Becky was quiet on the other end as I mumbled in frustration, just loudly enough for her to hear.

I was blinded by the anger, as well as the fact that I was taking it out on her. Like a strong, addictive drug, I was drawn to the anger's power and unable to resist the urge to lash out. Was this how my father felt when things did not go according to plan when vacuuming the pool? Or when he lost his temper with me during football?

She finally spoke slowly and softly, sadly showing decades of practice at calming me down. "Mike, if you would just—"

"PLEASE, Becky! Can you just help me get to the highway?" I could take no more and hung up the phone, largely because I knew that option was better than where I was headed.

Shit. I called her back. "Becky, I—"

She hung up on me. Becky had reached her tipping point.

There was a moment when I had an opportunity to make a decision. To either continue to feed off the anger that had risen to the surface or calmly face the feelings with mindfulness and with the one who loved me the most. I missed that small window at the time and found it impossible to course correct.

When I was finally able to gain some sense of control over my emotions, I called my wife back. It took a few tries, but she finally picked up, and I had gained just enough control over my volatile emotions to calmly ask for her help. She figured out where I was and how to get me to Highway 25. We spoke several times over the next few hours. I thanked her for her help, which was my pathetic way of saying "I'm sorry."

Sadly, I was unable to see how selfish and mean my behavior was at the time. I want to be clear that these moments of lashing out were not regular events, but they stand out painfully in my mind. I'm incredibly proud of myself as a dad and a husband, but I am not proud of these moments. Especially when they were compounded by my inability to say "I'm sorry."

Becky had witnessed my toxic storm cycle many times during our years together, and I'm grateful for her patience. In addition to the blind rage that occasionally consumed me, perhaps I subconsciously, or even consciously, took advantage of her steadiness, confident she would support me even at my worst. This journey has helped me discover this about myself, and seeing it clearly now, I see how unproductive and unnecessary all the rage is.

Despite losing it with Becky and losing my way while driving, the trip to Wyoming turned out to be uneventful. All the stress and worry about the highways closing never happened. In fact, seven and a half hours of the eight-hour drive had dry roads. It was not until I hit Hoback Junction that the snow started flying.

During both of the scenarios I described—the accident and getting lost—I was filled with explosive energy, but neither had any lasting emotional or physical suffering attached to it. Immediately after both events, I was nervously waiting for my body and soul to be affected, but it never was, and I didn't understand why.

But after attending the retreat at Kripalu and listening to Dr. Levine talk about how trauma energy needs to be released versus being held in the body, my conclusion was that because I was able to vent immediately after each trigger, that act of talking allowed me to release the energy so it could pass through me. Unfortunately, in the second scenario, Becky paid the price of my emotional release, which wasn't fair or right. I knew I still had a long way to go. Properly releasing my emotions was key. No one else should suffer because I was in emotional pain.

The trauma cycle was starting to make more sense to me. I always held things in, particularly when I became stressed, anxious, or angry, as far back as I can remember. I was slowly learning through my healing journey that expressing myself to Becky, and those I loved and cared about most, often improved my flow. And of course, it was clear that "expressing myself" needed to come out in different ways besides anger, which wasn't acceptable. Unfortunately, it was hard for me to always do that—even with that awareness.

Reflecting on the anger I'd felt while getting lost driving to Wyoming was also a portal to past anger episodes and allowed a slightly better understanding of myself. I can now honestly say that every time I've gotten mad at Becky, I was never angry with her. I was always angry with myself. This overwhelming—and at the time, unidentifiable—feeling was something I felt inside of me, rising to the surface, and that scared me. The only way I knew how to deal with it was by lashing out at the person I cared most about, Becky. I finally began to understand my anger and where it came from: my inability to process emotions.

I had recently read a book by Sharon Salzberg that Kaylee had given me called *Real Love: The Art of Mindful Connection*. In it the author shares:

> When we pay attention to sensations in our bodies, we can feel that love is the energetic opposite of fear. Love seems to open and expand us right down to the cellular level, while fear causes us to contract and withdraw into ourselves. Yet, so often, fear keeps us from being able to say yes to love—perhaps our greatest challenge as human beings.

Salzberg goes on to say, "Close relationships ask us to open our hearts and expose our innermost thoughts and feelings. Yet, if you felt unseen in childhood, the risk of self-disclosure can seem almost life-threatening."[20]

So, maybe I wasn't nuts after all. She pretty much summed up everything I had been experiencing. Perhaps I had felt unseen as a child. Like when my sister and I sat in the back of our car in silence after my father's road rage incident. Or when I tried to remain quiet to avoid his temper. Regardless, I could certainly relate to the risk of self-disclosure.

---

20 Sharon Salzberg, *Real Love: The Art of Mindful Connection* (New York: Flatiron Books, 2017), 116–117.

CHAPTER 22

The Second Arrow

A t the beginning of December 2019, my good friend Matt joined me in Jackson for five days of early-season epic ski conditions. Over the past few years, he'd also caught the powder bug and had become a damn good skier. We had a great time, tearing ass all over Jackson Hole Resort, and skiing a foot of new snow every twenty-four hours. During that time, I developed pain in my upper shin, just above the cuff of the ski boot and below the knee. For the most part it didn't bother me skiing, but it was becoming very painful at night. It was an injury I had never sustained before, and I was somewhat confident that it was TMS pain. I probably should have rested it, but since Matt was visiting, I wanted to be a good host and tour guide. So I continued to ski mostly full days, even feeling reluctant to talk about it with him.

Once the sky dried out, it was nice to head home and see Jaimie and Becky. Although I was carrying some sort of lower leg injury, otherwise I felt good physically and emotionally. In addition to being excited to see the girls, I was looking forward to resuming my writing and my yoga practice.

Now almost two weeks since my skiing trip with Matt, the pain I'd developed in my shin and right knee was still with me. I tried skiing on the East Coast, but after a couple of hours on firm snow, trying to be mindful, I stopped. I also took a break from going to yoga because of the pain. Logic would tell me it was TMS, as the pain seemed to move around a bit. It had started in the front of the knee but had migrated to the back and then the side. Classic TMS. However, unlike my other TMS symptoms, my knee still hurt while I was active, even when skiing and doing yoga.

I worked hard to stay calm and present, but as the weeks passed with little improvement, staying calm proved difficult, and I started to retreat inward. While this inward retreat certainly was a better option than lashing out in anger, it was not healthy and certainly not any type of long-term solution. Not that I recognized that at the time. The lessons I had learned about the importance of opening up and communicating were often lost when I was in pain.

Becky had been encouraging me to connect with Dr. Stracks to get his opinion on whether he thought I had injured my knee or if he believed it to be TMS. I didn't want to talk about that with Becky, nor did I want to reach out to Dr. Stracks. My mood started to change, as did how I chose to communicate with Becky, or not communicate. It just seemed easier and less painful to remain calm, quiet, and alone.

I knew I was going down that same old rabbit hole, but I felt I needed to *control* the environment. And the only way I could assure myself of that was to remain silent. I mistakenly confused myself with what I was controlling and its purpose. I thought what I was controlling would provide me with safety and ease. But it was doing just the opposite. By trying to suppress my emotions and deny reality, I was adding fuel for my TMS symptoms of pain! And, as I was learning, any type of pain has a purpose, and if we ignore it, it will only get worse. No longer able to take the pain in my knee, I finally decided to talk to Dr. Stracks.

It was good to catch up with him. It was hard to believe it had been so long since we'd spoken. I'd always enjoyed our chats and shared with him what I could piece together about the knee pain I was having. He asked me questions about the pain and what I could or could not do.

I explained that I'd started to become more mindful of my body. I realized that I needed to listen to my whole body—*all* parts: emotional, physical, and intuitive. I'd learned this from reading philosopher and psychologist Eugene Gendlin, who referred to this idea as our *felt sense*. This is a sensation-based feeling and does not come to us in words, but rather in a sense. Think of sayings like, *I'm going with my gut. It's in my heart. I have a funny feeling inside.* This felt sense is how our bodies interpret the world around us.

I also let Dr. Stracks know I was trying to develop an open dialogue with my body, to be kind to it, and that often resulted in not pushing myself all day. I told Dr. Stracks I found it more difficult to listen to my body. I had been accustomed to spending a lot of time by myself recently and noticed that I'd gotten anxious when I'd been skiing in Wyoming recently and had worried about entertaining my buddy Matt.

I eventually realized this feeling had nothing to do with Matt. In fact, we had always flowed great together on trips, both on and off the mountain. As I was learning how to navigate my emotional world and triggers, I saw that these issues were about me and how I felt about myself. This all led to my struggles with listening to my felt sense on a consistent basis. While speaking with Dr. Stracks, I was able to explore whether I had been anxious about disappointing Matt or if I had been concerned about letting myself down on a deeper level. I mean, what would I think of myself if I hadn't been able to ski all day as usual with my good friend? So, once again, I was putting undue pressure on myself to perform.

After talking about my situation for fifteen or twenty minutes, Dr. Stracks concluded that it was most likely TMS pain. He said, "You just have a lot going on in your mind and, like in the past, you're still experiencing some of your emotions through physical pain."

I asked him what I should do. He told me to get back to being active, to being kind to myself, and to continue to listen to my body and my felt sense.

After the call, I noticed I was still off emotionally and had a difficult time sharing the results of the call with Becky. Because of that, I could sense some tension between the two of us. The next morning, while I was still lying in bed, Becky came up with two cups of coffee. After we sat in bed sipping our coffee, she broke the awkward silence and shared some of her thoughts and observations.

"You have no idea what a roller-coaster ride I've been on with you. Your struggles don't just affect you. They affect me, too. My world and our kids' world revolve around you. When you are in pain, we are in pain. We want you to be happy. When you suffer, we all suffer, and when you are sad, we are sad."

As I sat there listening, I thought, *Roller coaster? She was on one too? My entire family was on one? It wasn't just me?*

I realized she was right. One of my strategies, or defense mechanisms, with my physical pain or emotional suffering was to become silent. I had convinced myself this was better than becoming emotional and outwardly upset. What I failed to recognize was the effect this inward withdrawal had on my family. It never occurred to me that they would be in real, meaningful pain because of it.

That early morning deep conversation allowed me to address my inability to say "I'm sorry." It's always been hard, if not impossible, for me to do that. And I never understood why.

I tried to explain to Becky there was an internal wall preventing me from offering an apology. Something I was afraid of, I guess. What that fear was, I still didn't know. I went on to tell her that it was like standing on a pier over the cold Atlantic in the dead of winter. And someone told you to jump in the ice-cold water and that they would wrap you in warm blankets when you got out. You might stand on the edge of the pier, wanting to jump in and trusting you will be warm after, but something still keeps you from taking the plunge. The resistance is that powerful. And that's what it feels like for me. I suppose, down deep, I am scared of what will happen if I jump in and say, "I'm sorry."

Maybe I was afraid of being vulnerable. That is not a safe position to be in, which makes sense when I look back on my childhood experiences with my father and his volatile nature. Being vulnerable likely would have been risky. So, over the years I probably just built a wall to protect me from getting hurt. Ironically, that very wall that was supposed to protect me ended up causing greater suffering. This lack of expression (apologizing) only added pressure to my already overloaded system, maintaining that supply chain for pain.

Becky slowly started to grasp what I was saying, as well as the power of this wall I was describing. It felt good to get all this out in the open. I guess it was one less secret I was holding on to and keeping from others, myself included.

That afternoon, less than twenty-four hours after I spoke with Dr. Stracks and six hours after the big conversation I had with Becky, my knee pain improved by eighty percent. My sense was that both conversations helped me release stored energy, resulting in a major improvement in my pain levels.

The next day I had my scheduled call with Eric and shared with him what Becky had said—that I had no idea of the pain and suffering that she had been experiencing through my healing journey. After I was finished, Eric said, matter-of-factly, "Becky is two hundred percent right. You don't understand." I had grown to respect and trust Eric, so while I wanted to get defensive and say, "What the fuck are you talking about, Eric?" I remained quiet and calm, patiently waiting for further explanation. It seemed like an eternity before he spoke again. After a lengthy pause (perhaps he was waiting for me to chime in or wanted me to take a moment to really hear what he'd just said), he finally told me the reason I didn't understand was because I could not fathom that someone would love me so much, to care that deeply, that my suffering would or could affect their emotional well-being too.

It was a powerful statement, and I remained still for a moment. At first, I had a hard time wrapping my head around his explanation. While intellectually I was aware of how difficult this journey had been for Becky, really feeling it was a different story altogether. Both she and Eric were right. I did not fully recognize the pain I was causing Becky and my family. It appeared that it was not in my emotional toolbox. In fact, as I continued with my spiritual awakening and expanded awareness, it was becoming apparent that my emotional toolbox was limited and, at times, pretty empty.

The more I thought about their comments and recognized the truth in them, I also started to see this from a different angle. In addition to what Becky and Eric painfully pointed out, I now saw how selfish I had been and how I'd become so attached to my own agenda. I was so caught up in my own troubles that I completely failed to see how my actions and behaviors affected those around me—love or no love. If I was around the house in a bad mood, remaining quiet, of course that would affect others. I should have been able to see that.

I now see that pain actually isolates us, it keeps us in our own little universe. That's what the mind does. It focuses on the pain and by doing so, it allows the pain to grow and swallows us up in the process. I have learned the goal should be to widen our perspective, to zoom out, and to pull back from the pain to see the bigger picture. Meditation and yoga can help with that.

I was starting to see the different layers of pain and the effects they had on me.

There is both physical pain and physical discomfort. And there is the emotional pain associated with both. Looking back, I see at times the emotional pain was worse than the physical discomfort. It's the story I created in my mind regarding the meaning around the physical discomfort that created this emotional pain. It's like I was stuck in this loop, telling myself things like: "This sucks! Will it get worse? Why is it here? How long will it last? I can't be happy because of it! I don't deserve to be happy! I'll wait until it's gone to be really happy." On and on I went, only making the situation worse. But that's precisely how pain works!

In Buddhism, they talk about the *second arrow*. As the story goes, we are shot by an arrow and instead of pulling the arrow out to help with the wound, we grab a second arrow and stab ourselves. When we suffer, two things happen. First is the actual event, which often is painful and unavoidable. That's the first arrow. The next thing that happens is the suffering, representing how we respond to the first arrow and the stories we create in our mind. This is the second arrow, and I now see how optional that is. If we don't respond mindfully, I agree wholeheartedly with the Buddha—the second arrow is far worse than the first. But with mindfulness, we can completely avoid that second arrow and the great suffering that accompanies it.

It was as if I had been living under a dark cloud, unable to see beyond the small world I lived in. But as I did the work and the cloud slowly lifted, I recognized the pain I was causing Becky and our kids. Some incidents were pretty obvious, while others were more subtle. And while I never lashed out at the kids, through my practice of isolating myself, I unknowingly removed myself from their world, no longer present for them. As healing took hold, patience, listening, and simply being present for the family started to happen without effort.

The first time I noticed this change, we were planning a long weekend in Vermont. In typical fashion, I was outside by our car, ready for our prompt 8:00 a.m. departure, while Becky lagged, presumably still trying to find the right outfit. After about fifteen minutes and without fully recognizing what was happening, I suddenly realized that even though Becky was late for our agreed-upon departure, I wasn't anxious, angry, or frustrated. I just *was.* This may sound like a silly example, and admittedly it is, but for me, it was profound. As I sat comfortably outside on our front step, patiently waiting for Becky as the clouds drifted by, I absolutely knew something had changed in me for the better.

But not all situations resolve themselves so effortlessly, and I notice when I need to open my toolbox. When I get triggered, and impatience, anger, or frustration start to rise to the surface, I recognize the feeling, accept that it is there, and I don't fight it. And most important, I remind myself that it is impermanent. I then take a few slow, deep breaths and, if possible, figure out how I can move my body with yoga or exercise. I also often excuse myself from the situation, not to isolate myself, but rather to give myself another chance to take a few more breaths and center myself. It's taken a lot of work and time, but even Becky has noticed an evolution in my way of being. She has commented that I'm more patient, I rarely lose my temper, and I don't complain. And her fears over my pain have started to subside as well. For years, she would tiptoe into a room I was in, wondering whether I was sad, in pain, isolating, or . . . just reading a book. Thankfully, lately, she usually finds me reading a book.

CHAPTER 23

Being Present

Even though I was making breakthroughs and small discoveries about myself, I continued looking for answers and the deeper meaning behind each triggered event. And though I was starting to communicate better by sharing things with Becky, I still needed to work on that for her sake. I had come a long way on this front, but there was more to do. There was no question I was healing (except I'd forget that when I was triggered). The spikes in pain were more spread out and the bad effects did not last as long. In fact, as time went on, the triggered episodes were affecting me more emotionally than physically. I had been told by those who provided guidance through this healing journey that this was normal.

Eric told me that experiencing emotions for the first time can be very alarming. And he was right. After all, I was becoming unfrozen after a lifetime of bottling up my feelings. So, of course, the emotional struggles that followed a trigger were always tough for me to navigate. I never really believed that the struggles would end, which prevented me from seeing the light at the end of the proverbial tunnel.

Instead, I often thought I would feel this way forever, and it was overwhelming when my emotional pain surfaced. It felt wrong and foreign to me. As I struggled with my feelings on the path to physical healing, I began to wonder if all the emotional suffering would ever stop. When would this stage of healing be complete? Would I ever be able to process my emotions, so they did not affect my mood and physical body?

I recalled Dr. Levine's work from the retreat I'd attended at Kripalu. Perhaps I needed to notice the changes in my body, but then quickly move on. This would be more productive than letting myself get caught in the emotional vortex, so my body did not become frozen again, like the traumatized animals. Maybe the issue wasn't to avoid feeling pain, but rather not to freeze in the pain.

As if the whole thing was not bizarre enough, not only was I experiencing emotions of the present, but in startling fashion, I was also experiencing painful emotions from the past. One morning, I went to yoga and ran into an old friend who told me he was taking his family to Iceland for vacation. We chatted about it for a few minutes, as it's a place I would also love to visit. Once the yoga class started, I put it out of my mind. However, toward the end of class, while lying on my back in Savasana (resting) pose, my thoughts drifted to Iceland. From there, I thought about how great it would be to take Mikey to Iceland for a ski touring trip. I quickly told myself Iceland was too far from Montana where Mikey lived and that maybe I should take him to Alaska again instead. These thoughts were happening at light speed, and as soon as I thought of Alaska, I was overcome immediately with strong, powerful emotions from our previous trip.

With my eyes closed, I felt like I was reliving the buildup to our last excursion to Alaska, when the conditions didn't work out. It was startling, as if I'd jumped into a time machine and was transported back to that very moment of all-consuming pain as I tried to prevent my son's possible disappointment if conditions weren't perfect.

The only difference was that now, lying on my yoga mat, I finally understood that the reason behind what I was feeling then had nothing to do with the weather and Mikey. It was me (my pain-body), something deep inside me that was touched and triggered. Trust me, I know how silly that looks, to have that much pain and suffering over a lack of snow. Poor retired me. Yes, I know. All I can say is, the pain was very real. I recognize everyone's situations are different, yet we all feel frustrated or angered by circumstances beyond our control.

The moment on my yoga mat was powerful and alarming. In retrospect, I wish I had stayed with the experience longer to identify the core emotion I was feeling. In my mind-body work, I have learned that fear always masks something deeper. What was I afraid of? Was it disappointment or losing control? Did I feel overly responsible, even for the weather? Was *caring too much* an issue?

Shocked by the intensity of the moment, I wanted out of the experience. Quickly, I blinked my eyes several times and jerked my head forward like I was trying to shake the memory from my mind. And with that motion, there was complete silence. No emotions were still attached to those thoughts and memories. When I realized I was no longer in fear, something in my throat started vibrating uncontrollably and lasted about thirty seconds.

What was the tremor in my throat? Was Alaska a traumatic event I was releasing, just as Dr. Levine described?

A light bulb of sorts went off. With greater clarity, I knew I couldn't control the weather. Kids will be disappointed and that is OK. In fact, disappointment is healthy and builds resilience. Intellectually, I now knew all of this. Overreacting was just that, overreacting.

Days later, I sat at my desk and looked for more answers. I took a notepad out and started writing down all the times in the past when

I was triggered and had strong emotions of hurt around my kids. Soon my list filled up with things like fear of poor skiing conditions, seeing my kids being left out of friend circles, and witnessing their disappointment in team sports. It was a long list that took no time to build. I am not a dad who treats my children with kid gloves; in fact, I have no problem disciplining them when they do wrong. But what became abundantly clear with my list writing was *my* tendency to get triggered when I perceived my children's disappointment, sadness, or embarrassment. I felt their reactions (or what I thought were their reactions) and fed off them in an emotionally powerful way.

I then wondered if the pain I felt was really my pain as a child? Or was it the result of my children's disappointment and I didn't know how to process it as a parent?

After reflecting on this type of suffering and its trigger, I realized my worst fears were seldom realized. My kids were fine. In fact, as a family, we were all more open now. Perhaps seeing their dad talking freely about his emotions so often gave the kids a nod to do so as well? I see my influence on them—they're all open to meditating and we even started Thanksgiving by going to a group yoga class together! I wondered if this awareness would help my healing.

I recalled reading Buddhist teachings about life and its cycles. The sun comes up and the sun sets. There are good times and bad times. We are born and we will die. We get happy and we get sad. All very natural. Perhaps I needed to feel those cycles within my own body. And truly understand that life is full of cycles. I wanted to feel comfortable and safe enough so that during the bad times, I would cycle back into good times. But as Dr. Levine pointed out at the conference, when we are thrust into the immobility–freeze phase, we need to understand this is all involuntary, because it takes place in the primitive part of our brain and nervous system.

+ + +

After spending the holidays in Wyoming with the whole family and as New Year's Eve approached, Becky took Jaimie back to New Hampshire for school. As luck would have it (for me), the snow started falling the day after they left and continued to snow for the next fifteen days. We had eleven feet of snow in two weeks! After I experienced the first few days of fresh powder, I had some guilt about staying longer. But I talked with Becky about extending my stay in Wyoming and sent Jaimie a text, asking her if she minded. Jaimie replied in her usual, supportive way. "Dad, I don't mind if you stay, because I know you are out there having fun and pursuing your passions. Love, Jaimie."

During that time, I told Kaylee I would drive her car from Jackson back to Boulder while she was traveling with college friends over the winter break. I agreed to that before I realized it was going to snow for two weeks straight. Eventually, I found a two-day window of opportunity when the storm let up and I could do the eight-hour drive, spend the night in Boulder, and jump on a plane the next morning and head back to Jackson to pursue deeper snow.

Once I was a couple of hours out of Jackson, the weather cleared, roads were dry, and the sky was deep blue. It was a beautiful day for a road trip. Four hours into the drive, I was really enjoying myself. I listened to music, podcasts, and even experienced some silence. All were equally peaceful. While I had always loved road trips, the past few years they were often difficult for me. It was not uncommon for me to get blue during a long drive by myself. But not this day. I peeked at myself in the rearview mirror and confirmed I looked like I felt—happy with a slight smile on my face.

I became more interested in what was happening and observed myself from afar while asking myself questions: Why was this guy so happy? How was this happening? Would it change? I then noticed I was *present* and experiencing the moment. I was not thinking about the past or worried about the future. I was here and now. And it was pretty sweet. As I focused on the experience, I noticed thoughts start to flash in front of me like a neon scrolling billboard. Would I miss a powder day tomorrow? Why didn't a good friend join me when I invited him? Perhaps I should be home with Becky and Jaimie. Would the light sensations building in my right foot get worse and become painful?

Eventually I realized a pattern had shifted: I was no longer grabbing on to those thoughts and creating stories around them. They would pop up and then dissolve right away. They seemed to have no power over me. And better yet, it appeared as if it was not requiring any effort on my part.

This was new terrain for me, to accept something at face value, as is, rather than trying to make something out of it. It reminded me of my meditation practice. When I started meditating, I was hell bent on keeping my mind quiet and blank. I thought that was the point of meditation. To me, a quiet mind equals a peaceful mind. But as I spent more time meditating, I found my practice shifting, becoming softer, less restrictive. While in silent meditation, with a gentle focus on the breath, not actively allowing my mind to drift but not restricting it either, I was almost inviting a stream of consciousness. I would observe thoughts come into my awareness, I would acknowledge them, and then slowly, gently bring my focus back to my breath and let those thoughts dissolve into the air.

What I was experiencing on this long car ride was an extension of my meditation practice. I was understanding, for the first time, that thoughts are just that, thoughts. No more, no less. While real, they are not true. They had nothing to do with the present moment.

Excited, I tried a little mental experiment. I called it "David Letterman's Top 10 Things that Really Piss Off Mike Murray." It was quite the list. And you guessed it, not enough snowfall was on there! After running through my list of greatest annoyances a couple of times, the results were in . . .

And you know what? They were no match for this Buddha in training! I did not grab on to any of them. My breathing didn't increase, I didn't feel any anger rising, my hands didn't begin to sweat. On this long, slow, peaceful drive, I was living in the right lane, living with ease.

The last four hours of the drive were as enjoyable as the first four. And the next morning, I was on a flight back to Jackson, skiing deep Wyoming powder by midday off Teton Pass.

It was a meaningful experience, but what if the epic storm was playing on my ability to be so peaceful? *Son of a bitch, was that why I was at ease and peace, because the weather went my way?*

But you know what? I quickly let go of that thought, too.

CHAPTER 24

Storm Cycle

It had been nineteen months since I'd discovered Dr. Sarno's book. It had been seventeen months since I'd been diagnosed with TMS by Dr. Stracks and fourteen months of being in therapy with Dr. Eric Sherman. I had been practicing meditation daily for thirteen months and yoga for four. I also had read dozens of books, listened to countless podcasts, and attended several seminars and lectures on whole-body wellness. I'd begun putting my experiences on paper, hoping to help others. At this point in time, I had thought, or hoped, that healing would be compounding and the pace of it would be increasing.

However, that was not the case for me. The healing path is so incredibly difficult, I often wonder if I am still even on the damn path! The physical pain still existed and letting go of the conventional medical way of thinking still proved challenging. And of course, the emotional pain was often (and still is!) like getting a bucket of ice water dropped on my head when I least expected it.

Yet, it had been months since I had experienced a significant spike in physical symptoms. Healing is frequently recognized not by experiencing the moment, but rather by reflecting and seeing subtle shifts that have been made. With hindsight, it had been a while since my pain had any real sting to it. My last few triggered events affected my digestive system more than anything else, which was no picnic, but I realized I could be as active as I wanted with only a light fuzzy sensation in my feet and hands at times. During idle moments on the East Coast, my body sensations did change, but not significantly.

The ringing in my right ear tended to be more obvious and the sensations in my limbs a bit stronger. But with the help of meditation, yoga, and therapy, I was becoming calmer and more comfortable having negative physical *and* emotional sensations as part of my life.

I was proud of my baby steps. I was also being smart with how long I skied or hiked, willing to stop once I felt fatigue coming on—particularly emotional fatigue. Upon further reflection, I realized I was connecting with my felt sense!

One day, Becky and I went to yoga, but some of the poses were quite painful when my lower right leg was bent. Over the next few days, without fully recognizing it, I became quiet and somber. In my mind, I was simply trying to stay calm and be patient until the lower leg injury subsided, and I could resume my yoga practice and skiing on the East Coast. It was not until Becky asked me what was wrong that I realized I had been in a funk. She said that ever since I had been home, she thought I seemed sad.

After she left the room, I got up from my desk, moved to my meditation pillow, and closed my eyes.

I then experienced one of those rare moments of groundbreaking personal understanding—a fundamental shift in what you know about your reality.

Becky was right. I was sad and had been for a couple days now. *How could that be?* I'd just enjoyed the holidays with my family in

Wyoming and had a wonderful time doing what I loved with the people I loved. But she was right. *When did the shift happen?*

Deep in a meditative state, I realized it had occurred after returning from Wyoming and while attending yoga. I had walked out of that class disappointed my lower leg was not ready for yoga. But it was more than simply being disappointed by the fact that I would need to take time off from yoga. It reached deeper, to my core, all the way to my beliefs, touching my stored trauma of the past—all at an unconscious level.

I always understood that I took great pride (and enjoyment) in being active. That was nothing new. But what I realized while sitting in stillness was that the insecurities I carried with me and nurtured from an early age had manifested to a point where I created, in my mind and body, a story of who I was and who I needed to be. If I was not on the move, pushing my limits physically, who was I?

I always knew I liked to push myself. But what I was now seeing was different. I was starting to see times when those insecurities had forced me onto my road bike or surfboard or into the backcountry of the Tetons or some of the most remote areas of Yellowstone National Park. Then I remembered times when I'd slept in the back of my van, rather than allowing myself to experience the comfort of a hotel bed. And if I would be unable to do those things, well . . . I started to see how the feelings of inadequacy would quickly rise to the top, raw and exposed, and be too painful to experience.

I rose from my meditation with a greater understanding of myself and my fears. Those masked feelings of inadequacy pushed me, demanded action, and if I couldn't accommodate its request, I would suffer emotionally. I saw and felt the shifts in my body. If I was shut down physically, for any reason beyond my choice, be it a lower leg problem, shoulder pain, or sore groin, from the core of where the unconscious resides, I was completely overtaken and threatened by this. My body reacted as if it were being chased by the woolly mammoth, as I hid in the woods, hoping not to be seen as I reentered the all-too-familiar immobility or freeze phase!

At face value, this may seem like an easy issue to resolve. "Stop pushing yourself, Mike," I could say. But what I was learning was that it wasn't that simple, and there were multiple layers with conflicting messages in those layers. Some of the very things that could cause suffering were the same things that brought me immense joy: going for long bike rides that would keep me in the saddle for hours; multiple surf sessions in one day; multiday ski tours in Wyoming and Montana; hiking all day to catch small, native Wyoming cutthroat trout with my fly-fishing rod in complete isolation; even camping and living out of my van for a couple of nights in a row. All these things made me feel alive and well!

How would I know if I was doing these things out of joy and passion? Or if I was driven to do them because of the fear of having my insecurities exposed? The way I have masked those insecurities was by being active, relying on my physical body to validate myself.

Sorting this out in my mind was like untangling a fly line on the side of a meandering river. It's a slow process, and often the fly line becomes so tangled that after ten minutes of tedious work, you realize you're going in the wrong direction, and you have made it worse. You take a deep breath and start all over again, as the cutthroat trout rise out of the water right in front of you, seemingly aware of your inability to move forward. At times like these, frustration can seep in.

Yes, pushing myself beyond what my body wanted was now showing up at times as debilitating physical symptoms. But the other issue was the effect this had on my mind and emotional well-being if I chose (or was forced) to not move and sit still.

I was pushing myself when my body needed rest to avoid the intense feelings of inadequacy that showed up whenever I was still. I didn't know this then, but the realization surfaced while writing this chapter. I now understood why my symptoms were much worse whenever I was idle. Stillness was stoking the feelings of being *less than*. There simply was no question that being outdoors and being active were both joyful and gratifying. Being active outdoors is a powerful, complete mind-body experience and that was good for me. But these outdoor adventures were creating a persona, a shield to hide me from friends, family, everyone. This provided a great distraction from seeing a side of me that I thought was weak and lacking. Subconsciously, I believed this persona provided me with comfort, knowing my insecurities were hidden from those who could use them against me (as if those people existed).

Did I know I had these insecurities? Sort of. I mean, I knew about them, but I did not understand their depth, significance, or consequences. And I certainly did not recognize how they influenced my behavior to the extent they have. I thought I was doing the right thing my whole life, protecting myself from embarrassment. That's how I thought I was supposed to make it through life to succeed. It's really all I ever understood. *If they ever knew*, I often thought. I'm not suggesting I was a walking basket case, afraid of my own shadow. No, it was not that. But there was often a sense that something was lacking.

Little did I know, the only one I was really deceiving was me. As much as I was doing this healing journey correctly and absolutely knew I spoke my truth the first fifty-two years of my life, I had a part of it completely wrong.

The stories and beliefs I created about myself . . . I bought into them—every single one of them. I had developed this idea and created a story about myself early in childhood and it had snowballed from there. It became stronger as I *hardened* around these beliefs. Our thoughts are like food that we put into our body. For example, good food provides nutrition for a healthy body. Whereas bad food, or negative thoughts, creates angst and disharmony within.

What we tell ourselves matters, regardless of whether it is spoken or thought. It all matters.

These stories I'd created about myself had limited my potential in several ways. Most important, they limited my ability to consistently live life with ease. And they limited my ability to communicate my truth and awareness of my own reality. I could not express who I really was or wasn't.

Those beliefs had developed into the bedrock of my existence and thus became a self-fulfilling prophecy. I did not demonstrate any outward signs of extreme anxiety that would alert anyone. I was happy and had friends. I was a strong little boy (maybe too strong mentally), and I became a strong adult, even as I was able to hide this story from others. And while I certainly was not a gifted athlete by any stretch, my mental strength allowed me to rely on and maximize what physical abilities I had been given. I probably became overly attached to that strength over time, tipping the scale too far in one direction and taking my body out of its desired balanced state.

Those early years of panic of being called upon in elementary school were the same apprehensions I had in middle school, high school, college, and beyond. They're still here, though they have begun to loosen their grip on me as I *thaw out.*

My anxiety had prevented me from taking chances and trying new things. That core fear still lingers with me today. I see it in my reluctance to use GPS in the car, my resistance to use Uber technology for a ride, my hesitation to order something online, and even my refusal to use our new washing machine. You might say I am lazy. Becky has rightfully accused me of that, and I acknowledge there is some truth to that. But my inability or unwillingness to confidently move forward with tools an eight-year-old now masters comes, without question, from the deep-rooted fear, lack of confidence, and anxiety over making a mistake—with a touch of laziness on top!

There were a lot of things I should have learned but failed to in school. And I confused this with a lack of intelligence. That was a big mistake on my part. I often thought, *How can a dumb kid be so aware of what he doesn't know? Shouldn't I be unaware of all this if I really am that dumb?*

Those insecurities I had in first grade, fifth grade, eighth grade, and beyond were carried with me, fully embraced and protected— even when I played an integral role in building a multimillion-dollar business from scratch. If it were someone else's story, I would have said they were nuts. But it was mine, and it made complete sense to me.

My choice to retire at a young age was influenced by these very same insecurities. I have no regrets over my decision. I have taken advantage of my freedom by spending quality time with my wife and kids, as well as pursuing my passions in outdoor activities. I have been so incredibly fortunate. That I know to be true.

There has not been one single day where I said to myself, "I really wish I was back at work." Honestly, not one. There's no question that I have fully embraced the lifestyle I have now, but equally pow-erful, I now accept, is the relief I enjoyed from no longer having to experience the anxiety of being *exposed* at work. I now see that I was just burying my fears without addressing them. In short, I was a ticking time bomb!

It's fair to say that if we had not sold a portion of our company to the VC firm, I would not have retired, at least not then. The desire to relieve myself of the burden I carried would have still been there. But without bringing in a new partner, really "smart" ones, and not having the perception I would be exposed, I would have stayed loyal and committed to my two business partners and those who worked for me, and continued with the grind.

But once free of that burden of work—which now I see was only real in my conscious mind—I was allowed to enjoy a new sense of adventure with greater ease, or so I thought. It took me no time to embrace the freedom, money, and lack of structure in my life. But looking back, I see that retirement never fully relieved me of those insecurities. In fact, all I was doing was fooling myself.

I thought retiring would dissolve those insecurities, but I soon learned I was walking a tightrope. Subconsciously, I was thinking people would now only judge me based on how far I rode my bike, how many surf sessions I got in, and how many days I skied. But, it really was not about other people judging me at all. It never was. It was how I was judging myself.

Without understanding that, it was a constant quest to quell my insecurity. I did not know it, but retirement and being adventurous were just Band-Aids that would allow me to temporarily avoid the painful thoughts and emotions that I felt in my body. These thoughts and emotions confirmed the elaborate story I had created about myself, handicapping me along the way. This was all happening on a subconscious level. My inability to get in touch with what I was feeling and experiencing emotionally only contributed to my suffering by stuffing those feelings even deeper. What I felt in my emotional body as confirmation of my incompleteness was really insecurity in disguise.

CHAPTER 25

The Blister, a Reflection

During my healing journey, my inability to process difficult emotions has led to physical pain. Almost five years after my initial small hamstring pull, I saw how things began to unravel for me that cold, snowy day back in December 2016. I had always wondered why I had the hamstring pain. I mean, what set this is motion? Why did it happen then?

Let's look back at that day I arrived in Jackson Hole on December 4, 2016. The day of the blister. It all comes full circle. For a backcountry skier, a blister is bad news. And that evening, after telling Becky about my blister, I'd hung up the phone and was hit with a wave of panic. A blister could shut me down. The whole ski season was being jeopardized in the blink of an eye.

For the next nine days, while on my own, I monitored this blister as if it were life threatening. I continued to ski in the backcountry, but instead of being connected to nature and the joy the experience of skiing powder in isolation brings me, I was no longer in the present moment. I was now focused on altering each step to reduce the friction in my ski boot. In addition to that, each night I would take a picture of the blister with my iPhone and study it in bed, trying to determine if the blister was getting worse compared to the previous day's image. In hindsight, I was being completely obsessive.

Looking for a solution, I went to three different ski shops, two drugstores, and called a couple of friends for advice, all in an attempt to control this blister before it prevented me from missing a season of skiing powder. Yes, I was concerned about the whole season! For almost two weeks, the blister consumed my attention. I had fanatical thoughts on how it could derail my ski season—I was simply unable to regulate myself. I now realize through my healing journey that the body and mind can only take so much. Eventually, the *bill* for unnatural and unnecessary pressure ultimately comes due. My cup was full.

After two weeks of being stuck at DEFCON 1, and as Becky, Jaimie, Kaylee, and Mikey arrived for the Christmas holiday break, the blister finally showed signs of healing. The crisis had been averted, and I had missed zero days on the mountain. However, less than a week later, I developed that first small hamstring pull—the injury that started it all, but one that had seemed at the time to appear out of the blue. I couldn't explain it, nor could I tie it to any sort of physical movement I'd done.

When I'd originally met with Dr. Stracks in August 2018 and was diagnosed with TMS, we'd discussed the onset of my pain. He asked me what was happening in my emotional world before the pain in my body started. He told me, in his experience, something almost always occurs to "set off" TMS. He said the spark is typically an emotional experience, a tipping point of sorts. He explained that while there was no steadfast rule, this tipping point usually happens within five months or so of the symptoms showing up and often immediately before the pain.

At the time of the discussion, I struggled to find anything

meaningful that I could put my finger on. Shit, I was fifty-two years old, retired, and pursuing all my interests with the passion you'd see from a kid. How could anything be bad? But I now see that it was this small blister that finally pushed my nervous system completely out of balance. A system that was overloaded. The blister was the proverbial straw that broke the camel's back. I remember distinctly how quickly I started to panic, all because of a little blister. My world and my worth had become threatened, and unbeknownst to me, unconsciously I reentered the freeze–immobility phase. For a blister.

My thinking during that "Week of the Blister" had become so narrow. Nothing existed outside of the condition of the blister and its effect on my ability to move in the snow. Looking back at it now, it's shocking that I couldn't see how dysfunctional I became. How did I not recognize those frenzied moments when I was in them? It's obvious to me now that something was very wrong. Yet I had no one to help guide me out of the *trance* and into clearer thinking.

This was the beginning of a chain of events that would take me on one hell of a ride. All the anxiety, emotions, and tension that had built up over that week obsessing about the blister needed to be released. Now that I know that when I'm unable to process uncomfortable situations and emotions they will manifest in my body as physical pain, I realize that hamstring pain solidified the nasty, self-sustaining, painful feedback loop—a loop that would take me over two years to break.

After the conveyor belt of doctors started—seventeen specialists in sixteen months—most recommended physical therapy, which always seemed like a Band-Aid, but I took the prescriptions and dutifully showed up at my appointments. The doctors who recommended some sort of invasive procedure were *always* more confident in their suggested treatment, as opposed to those who simply said I'd be fine. And the ones who told me I would be fine offered up no explanation for the pain. I always felt alone and hollow leaving those appointments. I craved certainty and despised ambiguity.

It wasn't until I met Dr. Stracks that I would see a path forward with a compassionate doctor who *listened* to me. And this relationship would prove invaluable.

CHAPTER 26

More than a Machine

Dr. Stracks was the last doctor I saw for my pain. I opted not to have any more surgeries or injections. By the time I'd scheduled an appointment with him, I'd rejected conventional diagnoses and embraced the mind-body connection and how it related to my pain. While I still experience sensations in my limbs, subtle ringing in my left ear, and triggers that occasionally take the light sensations across the threshold to painful, I have without question improved and not worsened, as most of the so-called experts had suggested would happen. And I have accomplished this through difficult inner-body work, while maintaining my active lifestyle to the fullest, albeit with slight modifications as it relates to listening to my felt sense. When I do have those moments when sensations change and become pain, I now understand something is out of balance and I need to do some work. These moments remind me that I need to pay attention to what is happening in my emotional world. I need to listen and care for my mind and body in a way that works for me.

Pain is a way the body is telling us that something is wrong.

And what is wrong is not always physical! We just need to understand that we are more than a machine. We are also emotional beings, and those emotions directly impact the health of our bodies in all sorts of ways. If you take a moment to think about that, it's quite astounding.

Most of the doctors I saw, unbeknownst to each of them, put the fear of God into me with their imaging, technical diagnoses, and fancy white lab coats. These doctors were not responsible for my original hamstring and shoulder pain, nor were they responsible for the trauma held in my body, but they played a major role in promoting the fear and anxiety I had been carrying with me and did nothing to help me with that (not to mention most were simply wrong with their diagnoses and conclusions).

Instead of listening and hearing what I told them about my anxiety, they were hell bent on interpreting the most recent X-ray or MRI before darting off to their next appointment. Instead of receiving care from those medical providers, I left each appointment in worse condition, both physically and emotionally, than when I had arrived. It often felt like I did not even need to attend the appointments, because there was no open dialogue between us. I was listening to the experts, but they were not listening to me or asking the right questions.

Without knowing it, each time Becky or I shared my emotional struggles with them, we were one step closer to identifying the cause of all my physical pain, but instead of taking the valuable information we provided about my overall condition, they ignored part of me, including my cries for help. Only one doctor briefly mentioned that emotions can play a role with pain. The rest seemed to believe that emotions have no impact on the physical body. They saw me as a machine that was broken. This perspective only magnified my fear and pain.

Western medicine has clearly lost its way, enamored with technology and the increasing clarity of sophisticated imaging. In the book *The Hidden Psychology of Pain*, Dr. James Alexander explained that about five centuries ago, the body began to be viewed by the Church as an imperfect vehicle for the transmission from this to the next world, known as mind-body dualism. This is the belief that the mind and body are separate. Then, as science emerged, the human organism was viewed more as a machine. In Western medicine, illness is still usually seen as separate from a patient's mental well-being.

The advances in science and medicine clearly have their place and have had a positive, meaningful impact on many people. And that is a wonderful thing. But from my perspective, advancements in imaging technology and cutting-edge medical treatments have been leveraged too far. Technology is great if it gives the doctor an advantage when treating the patient. However, this has resulted in an overdependence on technology and an underutilization of many other tools that help establish an understanding of the patient as a whole, such as the role emotions play in illness, injury, and disease.

Clearly, we all know emotions can affect the body. Consider when a young boy blushes when talking with a girl. When your stomach hurts right before an exam. When you get dry mouth before a big public speaking engagement. The mind has physical manifestations. And the body has mental manifestations. Just look at the effect on your stress level after exercising or a walk in nature. Or how your anxiety dissolves after yoga. Or how eating when hungry makes you less irritable.

Medicine must no longer separate the mind from the body when treating patients. Doctors must understand the whole person. So, in addition to asking a patient about the pain in their knee, for example, a doctor should ask what is happening in the patient's emotional world. Even at the most distinguished hospitals in the United States, doctors tend to ignore what the patient has to say about what they're feeling, despite the ever-increasing data that clearly show emotions play a significant role with pain and disease. This is a major reason for failed surgeries, the opioid epidemic, and the mental health problems of so many. I am not suggesting doctors do any of these things with malice, but I am saying they have a responsibility to treat the whole patient and not just a piece.

Medicine has become so incredibly specialized, there's a different doctor for each body part. As if each part wasn't connected to the next. And as if pain wasn't related to emotions.

To treat the whole patient, physicians must spend much more time with a patient than they do now. It will also require that the physician has adequate training in the mind-body connection and that they know how to communicate this idea effectively to the patient.

This would be a major shift in how doctors are trained today. Even if these things did happen, there would still be a lack of awareness and acceptance by the patient that the mind can have a major influence on pain, illness, and disease. In my experience, few people want to hear that their pain is psychosomatic, or they have a mental health issue. The physician will need to communicate this delicately, with a clear and full explanation about pain. And not everyone will be receptive.

Though there appears to be a subtle shift in medicine, and many doctors say they are embracing the mind-body connection, dualistic health care is still prevalent within our medical community. Each doctor who ignored what I was sharing with them was unknowingly validating this separation.

One of those times occurred when I was living with pain but prior to learning about the mind-body connection. Becky and I were seeing a spinal surgeon in Boston for a second opinion. While in the waiting room, as I paced back and forth because I was so nervous, Becky asked me to read something that the hospital had put up on the wall.

The quote came from one of the most impactful books I would later read in full: *Explain Pain* by David S. Butler and G. Lorimer Moseley. The hospital had pulled a page out of the book and hung it on the wall for patients to read. The excerpt was titled "Thought Viruses." It explained that when we are cut, nerve impulses run from the leg to the spine and then the brain, where the brain makes the decision to create pain (or not).

Similarly, our thoughts and emotions create the same type of impulses, which are sent to the spine and brain and initiate pain. The authors go on to say that humans, unlike nonhumans, can plan for the future, learn from experiences, and identify dangerous situations. So, when the whole human system is sensitive from anxiety or stress, for example, inputs (or thought viruses) can be interpreted by the brain as dangerous and create pain. In these instances, chances are you won't realize that your brain has interpreted this impulse as dangerous; you just know that it hurts.

I kept reading about some of the more common thought viruses, which included things like—

- I'm in pain so there must be something harmful happening to my body.
- I'm not doing anything until all the pain is gone.
- We can put a man on the moon, so why can't someone just fix this pain for me?
- I'm so frightened of my pain and of injuring my back again that I'm not doing anything.[21]

---

21 Butler and Moseley, *Explain Pain* (Adelaide, Australia: NOI Group, 2015), 81.

On the surface, this seems like a great thing to share. Here we have a forward-thinking hospital explaining how emotions can cause real pain through thought viruses. The only problem was, the doctor I met that day apparently did not subscribe to this philosophy or perhaps never got the memo. He just wanted to numb my pain with another injection.

Doctors need to listen to the patient, but they also need to be willing to engage and ask questions. Recently, an old college friend asked me to go out to lunch. He had hip pain, and his doctor was recommending a hip replacement based on the arthritis seen on the imaging. Knowing that I'd recently had a hip replacement, he wanted to talk with me about my experience and how I was doing. (He was not aware of my experience with mind-body pain.) We agreed to meet at a local Mexican restaurant not far from my house. As I drove over, I spent time thinking about the conversation I was about to have with him.

I wanted to help my friend. Kevin was a good wingman in college, and I know he had a difficult upbringing: alcohol and divorce in his family were just some of the things he dealt with when he was a young boy. I didn't know much about his situation other than what he'd told me via text. I wasn't sure if the pain he was experiencing was a mind-body condition, but I wanted him to be aware that there was another possible explanation to his pain.

Over the past year, I'd found myself in several conversations with other friends, talking about the mind-body connection as it related to their or someone else's pain. They were all happy that *I* was feeling much better, but they usually couldn't make that same connection to their situation of pain. So I was unsure how Kevin would view my take on the situation, and I certainly did not want to come across as a know-it-all.

I arrived first. Kevin rolled up moments later on an old, blue, beat-up motorcycle. As he turned off the ignition and took off his helmet, I wondered if he would ever get that thing started again. We each ordered burritos and I got a cold beer. Kevin was always a happy guy in college, but his smile seemed strained.

He said, "Mike, how's life been with a prosthetic hip? I've been putting this off for so long, but I think I need to bite the bullet. Thing is, I'm so damn nervous about it all. It's a big deal! How did you do with surgery and recovery? Was it terrible?"

I looked at him and said, "Honestly, Kevin, surgery wasn't bad at all. Recovery was slow the first couple weeks, more from just being really tight, but after that, progress happened pretty quickly."

His shoulders relaxed. "Well, that's good to hear."

I shifted gears and asked a few more questions about his pain and diagnosis.

Kevin tensed up and began to frown. "Mike, it's bone on bone. I saw the X-ray. Was yours like that?"

"Yup," I told him, trying not to make a big deal out of it.

Then he said, "My limp is terrible, and it's so embarrassing. I can't believe I am going to need a hip replacement at fifty-two years old."

I took a sip of my beer and asked, "What did the doctor tell you?"

Kevin said, "I've seen two doctors over the years and the most recent one told me that I am five out of ten in terms of needing a hip replacement or not."

Five out of ten. My heart sank. Such a nonconclusive diagnosis to depend on for a major surgery.

Determined to dig deeper, I asked, "How long have you had the pain?"

"It's really been my whole life, as long as I can remember. It's as if my hip's been dislocated and then fixed, over and over. But then there are times when there is no pain."

I thought about a big hike he and I did in Wyoming four years earlier when he visited me. It was a full-day affair of hiking and he never mentioned any pain, nor did he seem compromised.

I took a healthy gulp of my Corona and thought more about what he'd told me. It's possible that he had arthritis in his hip as a young kid, but highly unlikely. More probable, the pain in his hip was from the stress of family life when he was young, the stress that he probably still carried with him in the form of stored trauma. And that the arthritis found in the imaging was simply an incidental finding. I knew there were many case studies that showed that arthritis did not have a strong correlation with pain, because they have found arthritis in many asymptomatic people.

I then told Kevin my story of pain and wove in the mind-body connection, including what I had learned and how past trauma can affect our bodies in a way that mainstream Western medicine has yet to fully embrace.

Kevin listened but looked at me like a deer in headlights. He did nod a few times, so I figured he was remaining open to the concept.

"*But*," I told him, "it's quite possible you do need a hip replacement."

"Why do you think the pain is there, Mike? Why the hip?" he asked.

I shook my head. "I don't know the answer to that. I wish I did. Perhaps our brains sense changes in our body from arthritis, for example. Those changes create sensations. Then the brain identifies those sensations as danger or weakness in our body and they are an easy place to send pain to. But that's just my guess."

I told him I could give him a couple of books to read to see if anything resonated with him. I was learning that the mind-body concept could not be force-fed. If someone was going to accept it, it needed to be on their terms. I could tell that, while he was very interested in what I had to say and understood childhood trauma, he could not let go of what his doctor had told him and what he had seen on the image: bone on bone.

I could definitely relate. And so many other people could too . . .

Before we wrapped up, I said, "You know, in addition to having my right hip replaced, I also have significant arthritis in my left hip."

"Does it hurt?" Kevin asked.

I shook my head. "It doesn't and it's bone on bone. I was told I would need that hip replaced over two years ago." I continued, "Well, it does hurt occasionally, and I know you'll think this is nuts, but that pain comes about when something in my emotional world is bothering me, and I hold on to it. Once I recognize what I am experiencing emotionally, the pain goes away."

My friend stared back at me, unsure of what to think. When leaving the Mexican restaurant, I realized how difficult it often was for people—myself included—to embrace and act upon the mind-body connection. I understood a massive shift in thinking needed to take place, and I hoped to play some role in that movement, however minor it may be.

CHAPTER 27

Acceptance

Four years after the Week of the Blister, I finally understood the layers of emotional issues I was dealing with. I had retired to escape the feelings of inadequacy I constantly harbored, thinking retirement would put an end to such feelings. I was sure they no longer would be an issue in my life once I didn't have the anxiety about being exposed. Yet those fears would still crop up over the next nine years. For the most part, I was able to manage those feelings and keep them at bay. That is, until the Week of the Blister.

The blister was the start of allowing things to become exposed. The blister was what touched my feelings of inadequacy. My unconscious mind would say, *If I can't push myself in the mountains, what is my worth?*

While on my spiritual path, I first saw retirement as a Band-Aid I'd put on my troubled emotions. But, in fact, retirement had put me on a path to explore the process of pulling *off* the Band-Aid that had been there for some time—allowing the wound below to be exposed in order to heal.

Without early retirement, I would have continued to focus on my work and ignore what my body was trying to tell me. Though I did not know it at the time, it was the blister that eventually allowed me to see my inability to regulate myself, letting me look deep within and see the emotional layers of my reality.

It's because of the blister that I was eventually able see my anger, anger I directed at others, but really, I was only angry at myself. Most important, I had recognized and could now change the fact that the only way I knew how to deal with my anger was to lash out at the one I loved the most—Becky. I can't begin to explain how liberating it is to have that understanding with such absolute clarity. I have become far more patient, compassionate, and understanding. I'm accepting when things don't go as I had hoped, even when I get lost in the car—just ask Becky! And it was the itty-bitty blister that allowed me to see my father in me—both the good and bad parts.

My father was a good man and cared very much for his family and community. But his anger and temper often got the best of him.

Did I develop my inability to regulate myself by observing him when I was a child? Or did I inherit this behavior through what Dr. Levine explained as epigenetics? Dr. Levine's last lecture at the conference I'd attended at Kripalu was on generational trauma. He believes that trauma can be passed from one generation to the next through what is called epigenetics. The alterations that result aren't genetic but epigenetic. This means trauma does not change the genes, but rather how the genes are read and interpreted. Any outside event that can be detected by the body has the potential to cause epigenetic modifications.

Dr. Levine went on to share a powerful story about a laboratory test done with mice. They took several mice and exposed them to the smell of cherry blossoms, which the mice liked. They continued with that testing for some time. The doctors then introduced, with the smell of the cherry blossom, an electric shock. Each time the mice were simultaneously given the cherry blossom smell and electric shock, the animals would become very agitated because of the painful shock. The doctors conducted the test over and over with the same results. They then bred two generations of mice and exposed each generation to only the smell of the cherry blossom. There was no electric shock. And with each cherry blossom smell, each mouse in each generation demonstrated the same agitation.

You could say this example proves the behavior was genetic. Yet the problem with that theory is the original mice did not demonstrate negative reactionary behavior until they were exposed to the electric shock. This mice study is a proven example that generational trauma is real—through epigenetics.

Perhaps my inability to regulate was a result of both epigenetics and simple observation while growing up.

I knew my father's yearlong stay in the hospital followed by two years at reform school, then time living with his aunt, all played a major role in his developing self-esteem and the beliefs he held of himself. I often wonder what story he created in his mind about himself. What was his anger really shielding him from? I can promise you this: It was hiding something very personal and painful for him.

I now see that every time he lost control and got upset, it was because something in his core belief system had been touched. Unable to regulate himself, scared of the emotion and what lay below, the only way he knew how to deal with it was through anger, yelling, and screaming. He knew of no other way. Of course, my father never understood this, but my understanding gives me greater compassion for him and the demons he unknowingly battled his whole life. He did the best he could with the cards that were dealt to him. He was a good man and a good father.

As Michael Wickett states in his book *It's All within Your Reach*, "Whatever you believe, with feeling, becomes your reality. You are the sum total result of all your belief systems to this moment. Your beliefs form a screen of logic or a screen of prejudices through which you see the entire world. You never allow in any information that is inconsistent with your beliefs, even if you have beliefs that are totally inconsistent with reality. To the degree to which you believe these things to be true, they become true for you."[22]

For me, the healing journey has been like learning a new language. Like learning any new language, for most people, this can be very challenging. For the first six months of my journey, I did not understand anything. It was as if I was sitting in a small bistro in France, hearing the chatter around me in a language I did not speak, as if it was background noise.

But when I did begin to embrace this way of communicating, I found that it involved finding ways to stay calm while learning how to respond to people and circumstances with mindfulness. It's about treating yourself with compassion and being honest and proud of who you are. It's about not keeping secrets, including recognizing actions that we deploy to protect ourselves and survive. It's realizing the stories we told ourselves really do matter, but not in the way we assumed.

Thoughts of anger and fear create real chemical changes in our body. How can that be good? When you are truly healing, you will be getting in touch with your own thoughts, feelings, and emotions. I realize how challenging this can be, but if you can become mindful, over time it becomes easier.

This process is about understanding that while there is a beginning to the healing journey, there is no end. It's a way of life. For the longest time I was threatened with that idea. But as healing took hold, the thought of having setbacks, while never pleasant, no longer terrified me. My understanding of the path I had traveled was

---

22 Michael Wickett, *It's All within Your Reach: How to Live Your Dreams* (Wheeling, IL: Nightingale-Conant audiobook, 2014).

starting to shape the road ahead. I was no longer searching for the *magic bullet* that would cure me. I was not afraid of being judged if I needed another hip replacement, and more important, I would not judge myself.

I will continue to strive for happiness and health, and I've come to accept and embrace my journey and lifestyle to the fullest. This is not to be confused with giving up on the work. Far from it. But there appears to be a new level of acceptance within me. *Acceptance* in Buddhism means you consent to the world as it exists. You don't resign yourself to it, but rather eradicate your suffering by aligning with the reality of the world. From there, you can move into your ideal future.

As I learned from reading, particularly books on Buddhism, life is an ever-changing cycle. Problems arise when we cling to things because we want them to last. Or we cling to an idea of what we want this moment to look like or what we want the future to be.

The Buddha taught that "the nature of reality is that all things are changing." Think of an icicle hanging from the roof of your house. As the daytime temperature warms, the icicle starts to melt, drip by drip, only to have the water refreeze that night, seep into the ground, or evaporate into the air. And the process does not end there; the water that dripped from the icicle will be recirculated over and over again into our environment.

Just like the icicle, our human experience has its own cycle with many peaks and valleys. What I've started to understand is that those who have an altered nervous system have an inability to effectively regulate themselves. When you have been traumatized at some level, you will struggle to cycle out of the difficult moment when the trauma first occurred, causing you to remain stuck in fight, flight, or freeze mode.

These survival modes come in handy when we are threatened by someone pointing a gun at us, but not so much when a friend does not return a text message, or a spouse simply questions the music you chose.

When I read my first book on breathing and the power it has to heal us of so many physical and emotional conditions, it certainly was not the first time I'd been exposed to that concept. But over time, the concept began resonating with me. I learned that deep belly breathing will place the stress-response system into a healthier balance by activating the healing power of the nervous system. I now see how essential a calm nervous system is. Without one, the deeper healing I needed would have been impossible.

Over time, breathing and meditation helped me. While they did not eliminate those moments where I was thrust into fight, flight, or freeze, they enabled me to see that my life, as with every human's, is ever changing. Some moments are significant, while others are incredibly subtle. But if we pay attention, we will start to see and experience those moments, and we can feel the quiet shifts in our body. It's all about learning a new language.

What started as a journey to eradicate physical pain in my body turned into a crusade to ease the emotional angst I'd carried with me for a very long time. So, instead of turning against the physical discomfort, I found a relationship with both the physical and emotional pain and its cycle. What a simple yet incredibly valuable lesson to embrace: impermanence!

I know that suffering is caused by our reactivity to a stimulus, our interpretation to the meaning of that event. And often, that interpretation is completely distorted from reality. Psychology speaks of two waves of experience. The first wave is the stimulus, and the second wave is how we meet that stimulus. Deep contentment is the space between those two waves when we get to choose how we respond. Meditation helps with that, creating space that allows you to not get entangled in the first wave. To get to that point takes practice, particularly when your system has been taxed, like mine.

Early in my journey, I experienced what happens when you try to meditate for the first time, when your system is very sensitive and overtaxed. It happened when I closed my eyes and was overcome with childlike fear in a matter of seconds. I would come to learn that while that experience was disturbing to me, it was also common, but not natural. Our natural human state is very comfortable with silence and stillness. But because of my anxiety and the concerns I carried with me, I was seldom in this state, which was only made more obvious in the quiet of meditation. That is why so many people struggle with silent meditation at first. When the mind is not used to being in the natural state of calm, it pretty much freaks out.

I was slowly learning through reflection on my life's experiences that our reactivity can indeed cease to exist. We can have distance between the first and second wave of experience. We can choose how we do or do not get caught up in the emotions of suffering. It's not that we can fully eliminate our suffering, but we *can* determine how deep an impact our suffering has on our system. Suffering is when we are contracted and closed. When this happens, we don't have enough space to hold our feelings without collapsing into them.

With this understanding, I was able to look back on a couple of past scenarios and see the meaning in what I thought were meaningless experiences. The first event was the one afternoon after I finished my yoga practice and lay down and was suddenly engulfed by sadness, loneliness, and fear. But these emotions didn't hurt. I felt as if I were witnessing them from afar. I now understand that the emotions I sensed were the first wave, and I had so much space that my response to these emotions did not come crashing down, drowning me in the second wave. I was so spacious in that moment; I was in a state of Nirvana.

The contradictory experience was the one that happened during yoga class when I was in Savasana pose, when I'd simply thought of Alaska and was suddenly overcome with powerful, painful emotions of the past. In that moment, my awareness was Alaska, the concept of Alaska, and the emotional tone of Alaska. I had no space to acknowledge that it was simply an unpleasant experience. I'd collapsed and became entangled in the emotions. I'd become tight and my worldview became narrow, tainted with despair.

Those two scenarios after yoga practice show the difference between being spacious and open versus contracted and collapsed.

Yoga definitely proved to be a powerful tool for healing. I started the practice initially for two reasons. First, to spend more time with Becky. And second, yoga was a way to exercise and feed my body. But as I continued on the path, I found that yoga was starting to help me heal my trauma and, to my surprise, similar experiences were becoming well documented.

The simple act of noticing what you feel inside promotes emotional regulation, which helps you to notice what is going on in your body. As I struggled with being triggered, thrust into, and getting stuck in fight, flight, or freeze mode, I found that yoga helped with that, teaching my body to flow into and out of that cycle.

Yoga is a practice of coming into a pose, holding that pose, and then releasing it. All the while, you are focusing on your breath to help regulate your nervous system. Holding a pose can be very challenging and intimidating. My instinct is to release the pose when it becomes too difficult. In class, muscles are stretched, sweat pours out of your body, and you may find that you tell yourself you've been in a position longer than you'd like. Perhaps your legs begin to shake, and you just want to release the pose. But as I learned more about the relationship between yoga and trauma, I began to challenge myself, to trust that the painful, difficult moment of the pose would soon be over. And when I made it through one pose, I would rest for a moment before I moved on to the next one, just like in life, navigating one challenge after the next. All it took was some breath work and determination to stick it out.

It's this part of the yoga process that teaches us, our subconscious mind, and our nervous system that everything will be OK. We cycle into a pose, and we cycle out. We may be triggered by a person or circumstance, but instead of remaining stuck, we learn through yoga that we can indeed cycle out of that difficult moment.

The effects of trauma make you feel stuck when you are triggered. But in yoga and meditation, you learn that sensations rise and then simply fall away. Not long ago while I was in Wyoming skiing, I redeveloped some knee pain. Disappointed, sad, and not feeling good about myself, I called Becky. Without realizing it then, my call to her was one of my first attempts to try to stay present and in the moment. And I told her how I was feeling without anger or frustration. I didn't take my unregulated emotions out on her, nor did I seek to remain isolated.

She calmly listened to my story of pain and once done, she said with compassion, and a tender voice "I'm sorry you're in pain, but it's just a moment. Sit with it. Don't fight it and understand this also will pass."

Before my healing journey, I wouldn't have been able to listen to what she was saying. I would have resisted her suggestions about sitting with the pain. I would have told myself that she had no idea what I was experiencing and because of that, I would be inviting myself to suffer even more.

But during that call, I was able to mindfully listen to her advice and embrace it on a deep level, which allowed me to cycle right out of the moment of emotional angst and, ultimately, the physical pain. It was an exciting and rewarding experience for me (and Becky!), as I could have gone either way. Instead of falling back into the vortex of suffering, which was the natural path for me, I was able to use the tools and knowledge I had gained to prevent that from happening.

How far I'd come!

CHAPTER 28

Learning to Listen

O ne of the many gifts I have received by walking the path was the joy of reading books. I never read as a child and read very few books as an adult. I found it difficult to focus on each sentence and to comprehend what I was reading. The diagnosis of dyslexia hadn't helped with that. So, I would become frustrated and bored. Now I find reading to be therapeutic and important to my healing process. Reading about others who have struggled with similar issues is validating and makes me feel connected.

With each book I read, I feel as though I am reading about my suffering, about what I have experienced in my healing journey, or what the path ahead looks like. There is always something I can relate to. This has made me realize I am not alone and that unnecessary suffering is everywhere. This is the kind of suffering that Buddhism refers to as *all-pervasive suffering*. It is the type that is self-inflicted. Like mine, this type of suffering often has little to do with the actual circumstances and much more with how we perceive and interpret those circumstances. In other words, it's that second arrow!

What I believe reading cannot do, though, is heal trauma. Healing is done through the body and deep within the subconscious mind and nervous system, not from the intellect. With that said, reading and learning do absolutely play a role. Reading has kept me on the path, providing me with light when there appeared to be only darkness. Reading has also given me the assurance that I walked in the right direction. But I also believe that at some level, the understanding we acquire through reading does seep down into the subconscious and helps promote growth, awareness, and resilience, all of which influences how we heal by allowing us to create more space and therefore to be more mindful of how we respond.

When describing to Becky or our kids a book I have just read, I often feel like Mikey when he would call home from Montana, telling me with great enthusiasm: "Dad, I just had the best powder day ever!" He seemed to have many "best powder days ever." I felt the same way with most of the books I've read. They've been real, moving, spiritual, learning experiences. Each one has been a true gift.

One of the most influential books I read was by Tara Brach, titled *Radical Acceptance: Embracing Your Life with the Heart of a Buddha*. She describes *radical acceptance* as recognizing what is happening inside you with an open, kind, and loving heart. In her book she states, "When physical or emotional pain arises, our reflex is to resist it not only by stiffening our body and contracting our muscles, but also by contracting our mind."[23]

That certainly was my experience, most likely for my whole life. But as I continued on the path, I became much more aware of what was happening inside. Brach went on to explain that we can get caught up in our mind, stuck in an endless loop, worried about how

---

23 Tara Brach, *Radical Acceptance: Embracing Your Life with the Heart of a Buddha* (New York: Random House, 2004), 26.

long the pain will last, as we also wonder if it will get worse, which can confirm our feelings of unworthiness.

I had physical pain because I was unable to recognize what was going on inside my body. The emotional struggle that was happening was my body's way of saying loudly, "Help me. I'm here." It was the emotional tug-of-war that was ground zero. Once I was able to access that emotional experience, I continued to struggle because of my inability to let go of my fears. I held on to them as if they were real and actually mattered. Those fears, I presume, exist for everyone and can be buried underneath many layers, covered up by our beliefs and actions. It can require deep reflection to access them. Meditation is an effective tool to look deeply at your emotional reactions and find meaning behind them, which is crucial to letting them go. As Brach writes, quoting Pema Chödrön, "Once the resistance is gone, the demons are gone."[24]

When learning this new language of healing, instead of doing the very things I should have been doing early on to help in that process, I went to great lengths to do the opposite. When triggered, instead of being physically active, I became passive. Instead of socializing with others, I sought isolation. And instead of sharing and communicating with those I cared about and those who cared about me, I retreated inward.

Those behaviors gave me a sense of familiarity, security, and control. While those decisions were never responsible for initiating a triggered event, they did drive me deeper into suffering and helped establish the negative, painful feedback loop.

The pull to withdraw and isolate from others is so powerful, yet it only makes the situation worse. Healing happens when we are feeling engaged and accepted by others. All too often I was *just waiting* for healing to occur. But time does not heal. Rather, it's what we

---

24 Brach, *Radical Acceptance*, 152.

choose to do with our time that can help us heal. Suffering happens from our attempt to avoid our deep emotional pain. But trying to block out what I was feeling only made the suffering stronger. Without embracing the pain-body connection, I most certainly would have never addressed my underlying issues that created anger, impatience, and false beliefs about who I thought I was. I can now see that I am blessed that my pain-body has spoken to me.

I learned about a term coined by Dr. Dan Siegel, *window of tolerance*. He described that as an optimal window with which we can respond to an event without becoming triggered. If we have a big ol' healthy window of tolerance, it means we benefit from having a healthy nervous system that enables us to respond to challenging experiences calmly, because we process these signals without becoming too reactive or withdrawn.

What I learned is there is also a faux window of tolerance. This happens when we develop defense mechanisms that allow us to trick ourselves into believing we are healthy and in that optimal zone. Defense mechanisms manifest in ways that are unique to each of us. They could manifest as substance abuse, excessive exercise, obsession with work, eating disorders, or the need to surround ourselves with others. They could be anything that provides a feeling of happiness and sense of control. It's when you are unable to be calm and relaxed unless you are doing those things that it then becomes a defense mechanism.

For me, early on, my defense mechanisms were isolation and being in Wyoming. And while there is something incredibly uplifting and healing in being in the mountains and clear streams of Wyoming, I believe I was operating in this faux window of tolerance, giving me a false sense of calm and ease.

Because of my personal growth, I've also started to recognize *tighter cycles* that often lead to great insight, understanding, and wisdom. This happened in the spring of 2020. After dealing with on-again-off-again lower leg pain for a few months, one day I noticed that the pain and sensations in other areas of my body had diminished. My glutes were now pain free, there was little tingling in my arms and hands, and while my feet still had moments of sensations, they were very light. Everything had improved—the opposite of what most doctors told me would happen unless I opted for surgery or had stem cell injections.

Excited about this observation one morning, I also noticed my lower legs seemed to have a greater flow to them as well. As I walked downstairs, I realized my legs felt even better moving. Instead of heading to the kitchen as planned, I proceeded to turn around and run up and down our staircase, mimicking the motion of a football player high-stepping his way to the end zone. After spiking the football, I donned my yoga knickers and headed to power yoga class. I felt great.

I returned home a few hours later with an immense amount of confidence and joy. But that changed as soon as I walked up the stairs. I was met with a sharp, throbbing pain that seemed to spider out from the center of both knees. I turned around and walked down the staircase pain free! *Phew.* But as I did a one-eighty and headed back upstairs, with each step, no matter how fast or how slow, I was greeted with this same sharp web of pain.

Devastated, I kept the intense pain to myself. The next morning, the pain still with me, I joined Becky for coffee but kept my knee pain to myself. As she read the newspaper, I tried to privately process what had just happened. I began to worry and contract inward, but I remembered Becky's powerful statement a couple of months prior, that I didn't understand how my struggles affected her. And she was right; her words had a lasting impact on me. I didn't want to hurt her anymore, so I tried to act as if everything was fine. And the real problem wasn't the new knee pain—it was that damn second arrow again!

After breakfast, I headed to my writing room and sat on my meditation pillow. I realized that I really, really didn't want to suffer anymore. Of course, I had never wanted to suffer emotionally, but this realization was different; it was deep and significant. I felt this message in my body. I sensed my body was asking me to take control. My body was saying, *Now, it's time, you are ready!* I didn't like how I felt when I suffered, and I didn't like how it affected those I care about. I saw that I no longer enjoyed the *power* of anger. I wanted nothing to do with it. I saw how anger and fear took me out of the present moment. And then the breakthroughs started happening. As I sat there, I realized that all we have is the present moment, since the past is no longer, and the future is yet to be.

As I processed my thoughts, I clearly saw what was happening; it was my reaction to the new knee pain that could cause emotional trouble for me and those connected to me. As I sat longer in meditation, I was aware of a deep sense of ease coming over me. Unconsciously, I started repeating a phrase in my head: Tomorrow is another day. Tomorrow is another day. Tomorrow is another day.

I thought to myself, yes, I have some knee pain but that's OK. Tomorrow is another day, and this knee pain very well could be gone. But if it's not, that's OK too, because who knows what will happen the day after that or even the day after that. What I did know for certain is that no matter what happened with the knee pain, I was way better off without sticking myself with that damn second arrow!

CHAPTER 29

Telling My Story

It should have been clearer to me how important communicating was to create harmony in the body. There were so many times, before and after I learned about TMS and the mind-body connection, that my pain diminished when I socialized and shared my experiences and feelings. I simply failed to see that connection. It really was one of the hardest things I had to learn to do—talk when I was in pain.

Talking was the last thing I wanted to do. During those episodes, most of my conversations were with myself and always fear-based. They were typically pretty simple and seldom was there any sort of meaningful reflection. I'd ask myself things like "Will this pain get worse?" and "Now what?"

But as I slowly began to trust myself and open up to others, I felt amazing relief. I just needed to be willing to show myself some compassion.

The conversations I had with Becky were always the polar opposite of the ones I had with myself. The talks with her were less negative. I spoke the truth, and by doing that I learned that the *self* needs to be heard to release the pent-up emotions and thoughts from the body. When I was stuck, if I could find the strength and courage to communicate with Becky, it was often my words and my voice that provided the relief. That is not to diminish what Becky had to say or her ability to listen intently, both of which were incredibly important. But my voice was like a valve opening, releasing all this powerful, built-up pressure.

Leila Levinson wrote that "Telling our stories helps us heal. The process of piecing together and sharing that narrative releases some of the energy created by the experience and allows us to externalize that experience, moving the emotional energy outward."[25]

I started this project to help others. And I have eagerly carried that torch with passion and commitment to introduce the mind-body concept to others in the hope that people would consider the mind-body connection before undergoing any type of invasive procedure or taking prescriptions to kill pain. I knew this story needed to be told.

But I now see that the writing itself allowed me to get to know myself in a very deep way. I was able to identify certain behaviors, beliefs, and tendencies. My decision to write my story was one of my first attempts to remove the self-imposed shackles and it came deep from within. I had been holding back for so long. No one told me to be quiet. It was a decision I made early in life, and I simply was never able to overcome that on a meaningful level.

When I finished this book, the very words I chose to put on paper came back to me with more impact and meaning, allowing

---

25 Leila Levinson, "Can the Simple Act of Storytelling Help Them Heal?" *Huffington Post*, January 9, 2012, https://www.huffpost.com/entry/ptsd-veterans-writing_b_1078971.

for greater insight and learning after I studied them again and again. By telling my story, I discovered the healing process of writing. It allowed me not only to express difficult emotions, but to also access positive ones. It gave me a sense of pride and an opportunity for growth. Reading my story allowed me to truly see where I was hiding and why. The process of writing gave me great confidence and filled me with passion and compassion. It showed me who I am and the gifts that I can bring to this world, one page at a time.

Top Down, Bottom Up

fter working weekly with Eric in therapy over twenty-four months, I paused and reflected on the work we had done together and the progress I'd made. He provided me with concepts and structure and then helped me see my triggers and put meaning behind them. He introduced me to the concept of trauma and the effects anxiety can have on your ability to learn as a child. Eric helped me understand that many of the false beliefs I'd held about myself were a mirage, a result of protective behaviors of the past. We talked about the implications of letting those beliefs move you around and dictate your actions in life. Our work together was inspiring at times; it also could be very light with lots of laughs.

I realized that I needed to start talking it out and working through the verbal content. Doing this helped me recognize that something was awry besides the physical pain. The process also revealed to me the importance of communicating and the impact it had on me.

Our sessions were cerebral, analytical, and above the collarbone. As is often the case, I entered the healing journey through my head.

It was during our work together that I eventually saw a much deeper level of the mind-body connection and what path I needed to take to continue to heal and grow.

I understood this connection was the bridge, the bridge from the mind to the body. And Eric was the first step onto that bridge. Our work together is what some people refer to in psychotherapy as a top-down approach. We were working with parts of the brain associated with thinking, speaking, and current emotional awareness: the neocortex (part of the brain's cerebral cortex, the top of the brain) and prefrontal cortex (part of the frontal lobe, the front of the brain). This work is about creating a change in your thinking that will produce a positive change in your emotions to positively affect your body.

This approach has worked for me, but I wanted to continue to move the football down the field, and I felt as if I was being drawn to something else, to the next stage in my liberation. I kept coming back to Peter Levine's work of Somatic Experiencing and the concept of releasing trauma through the body. What I found through my research is, there are many modalities that speak to the idea of letting go of trauma, and Somatic Experiencing was just one of many that work with the body. That type of work is known as a bottom-up approach.

This approach works with the parts of the brain located toward the base. The reptilian part of the brain is responsible for reflexes, memories, and automatic survival responses. If we reduce and remove the stress in the body, this will have a positive impact on emotions, which, in turn, will improve a person's thinking, reduce their inner conflict, and, potentially, lessen chronic pain and yes, even disease. This approach believes that it happens in the body first. With all the work I was doing with yoga, meditation, and observing the reactions in my body when triggered, this bottom-up approach very much resonated with me. But I was unsure how to begin this practice.

Becky—who was well aware of my curiosity with *held trauma* in the body—suggested I check out a yoga teacher online, Kali Basman of Kali Durga Yoga, who is unique in offering physical asanas combined with Buddhism, as well as deep psychological healing methods. I sent an email to Kali, introducing myself, the story of my pain, my struggles, and the path I had walked. I asked her if she provided guidance or mentorship on the type of journey I was on.

That afternoon she returned my email:

Hello, Mike.

I am honored to hear from you and of the incredible insights you've had over the course of your healing. It's evident how far you have come in the self-reflective process already. When the mind-body system wakes up after protective dormancy for many years, it's not only natural for the intensity of sensation to overwhelm the organism, but it also demonstrates the turning back "online" of your own body's inherent wisdom. Exiled parts of your personality structure, which may have gone into hiding to protect you in your younger years, are asking for integration. I see a pathway forward of much growth and wisdom for you, and I'd be honored to support.

See you on the path, Mike!

In solidarity,
Kali

PS: I also share your love for Wyoming. I spend some time there rock climbing when I'm able to. So glad you have that space to feel your wholeness.

+ +, +

From the moment I read her email, I knew she was perfect for me and exactly what had been missing in my mind-body work. As Eckhart Tolle says in *Stillness Speaks*:

A true spiritual teacher does not have anything to teach in the conventional sense of the word, does not have anything to give or add to you, such as new information, beliefs or rules of conduct. The only function of such a teacher is to help you remove that which separates you from the truth of who you already are and what you already know in the depth of your being. The spiritual teacher is there to uncover and reveal to you that dimension of inner depth that is also peace.[26]

The next day I had my scheduled call with Eric and shared with him my decision to stop therapy with him. I told him that I was going to start working with a yoga teacher and pursue the healing work that can accompany it. We talked about my decision, and although I know it didn't have to be a choice between Eric and Kali, I felt a fresh start would be beneficial. He was supportive and believed I would get a lot out of that type of work.

Though Kali and I conducted our sessions together on Zoom, it took me little time to realize that she was warm, compassionate, and full of wisdom. Over the course of the first month, in addition to talking about Buddhist teachings, we practiced and discussed mindfulness methodology and talked about the current medical research on neuroplasticity—that the brain has the ability to change and grow over time. She also included trauma-informed process and deep contemplations. All to support the healing of the nervous system.

We worked together using an evidence-based model called Internal Family Systems. It's the view that the mind is made up of relatively discrete subpersonalities, each with its own unique

---

26   Eckhart Tolle, *Stillness Speaks* (Novato, CA: New World Library, 2003), IX.

viewpoint and qualities. We also worked on cultivating my meditation practice—the process of taking an interest in the inner life. We focused on deep belly breathing and centering, as I dedicated myself to the practice of awareness for my own and other people's benefit. And she helped me develop a Yin Yoga practice. Yin Yoga consists of long-held poses on the ground. It is designed to stress connective tissues and fascia to improve flexibility, release tension, and hydrate tissues. Holding poses for three to five minutes allows you to release deep patterns of holding.

Kali turned out to be much more than a yoga teacher, or at least what I perceived a yoga teacher to be. I am sharing my experience with Kali because of how transformative an experience it has been for me. This is coming from a guy who up to twelve months ago never even considered practicing yoga or meditation. Unless it was in my wheelhouse (skiing, surfing, fly-fishing, and cycling), I deemed it to have little value. I admit, I could be quite the cynic. But something very real and deep was happening each week with Kali. Something even the most hardened cynic could not ignore.

After a few weeks of working with Kali, and my now daily Yin Yoga practice, I started to notice quiet changes. I felt as if I were moving around the house with greater ease. If the air had offered resistance as I walked, it no longer did. My sleep patterns started to improve, as did my energy throughout the day. I even had fewer pee breaks in the middle of the night.

While in the Yin Yoga poses, I noticed my body beginning to wake up. At times I would experience uncomfortable, nervous energy in my upper right leg while in butterfly pose. There were times when my face would get very warm or I'd feel pressure between my eyes. I would often feel twitching in my butt cheeks as well as the top of my knees, thighs, or backs of my hands. And while in Savasana pose, I experienced the sensation of an ant walking down my face. Kali says all of this is an indication of the mind-body connection starting to work, to awaken. I was experiencing a heightened awareness of my bodily sensations.

Most of these sensations were neutral, though I had a period of two weeks while working with Kali, practicing yoga, when I would have what I can only describe as a dark-gray cloud of pain that swept down my lower left leg. Never stopping, always slowly moving from the top of my shin to my ankle, and then out my foot. It was there suddenly and then slowly, it would go. This cycle would go on for five minutes, the sweeping pain repeating about every ten seconds. I would do my best to stay with the pain as it arrived, gritting my teeth, knowing (or sometimes hoping) it would soon pass. It almost felt like a test, that my body was asking if I was able to stay with that cycle, helping me reinforce the nature of impermanence.

What I learned along this healing journey is that everyone's experience will be different. Our experiences cannot be replicated. We are all unique and our bodies speak to us in different ways. The sensations I was feeling while in deep Yin poses were how I experienced my body opening up. Yours may be different. And as my work with Kali continued, I started to experience awareness in the body in different ways.

First, while sitting in silent meditation with my hands resting gently on my lap, suddenly and uncontrollably, my right arm jerked up into the air and over my head. It was quite shocking. By working with Kali, I learned that a deep meditative state allowed for an opening of energy that moved the blockages or trauma out of my body.

Then one day, after forty minutes of Yin Yoga, while in Savasana, lying on my back, feet on the ground, legs bent, knees touching each other, I noticed my right butt cheek trembling. That vibration slowly included my entire right leg and ultimately led to both legs and butt cheeks trembling. That first experience lasted for fifteen minutes and continued to happen every day as I practiced yoga. Over the next few weeks, the intensity of that trembling increased, as did the duration of the experience. It was as if I were a lucky antelope shaking off a narrow escape from a lion in the Serengeti!

For me, Yin poses paved the way for a release. After each session, I would lie in Savasana and that is when I trembled, releasing deep-held patterns of obstruction in the form of stress, tension, and trauma, facilitating the process of bringing my body slowly back into a state of balance. The experience of releasing this energy was calming. I was never nervous or threatened. I was at ease and fascinated at the same time.

But not all trauma release looks like this. I was learning it could be experienced a number of different ways: trembling and shaking, but also by crying, a deep sense of emotion, or even flushing of the skin. It's important to not have any preconceived idea of what it would look like for you. I would imagine reading about an experience like this could be alarming to some, but trust me, it's not. My body was doing simply what it needed in order to heal.

All the work I did has led to me to where I am today. I have learned that life is full of cycles, all of which are impermanent, and that the healing journey never ends. While I now feel incredibly grounded and confident, I, like every human, have struggles, but I am learning not to resist and hold on to those moments. When I am triggered and have a spike in pain, in addition to having the positive effects of a more balanced nervous system, I have also acquired the tools to manage the reaction to whatever life throws my way. And I continue to learn to be at ease with "what is." The sensations I have in my body at times are now seen as a pleasant reminder for me to stay connected to my mind and body; to be aware of what is in my emotional field is truly a message from my mind via my body!

I am enjoying my quiet time and remind myself, when I forget, to embrace each deep breath like it's a tall glass of ice-cold water on a hot summer day. I ski, hike, bike, fly-fish, and surf. I do what I do, when I want to do it. But now I listen. The days when I change my plans and decide to rest, that is usually a result of not the body or the mind speaking, but rather the combination of the two. It is my felt sense, and when it says I need to rest, I try to listen.

My body and mind no longer experience my time in New Hampshire any differently from my time in Wyoming. It's as if I have come home to myself. Home is a state of mind *and* a state of body.

Acknowledgments

I am forever grateful for the many who have supported and guided me along my healing journey, as well as those who have helped me bring this book alive—they were often one and the same. The four years it took me to write this book were incredibly challenging, yet also wonderfully rewarding.

Thank you to Nadia Colburn for helping me get the project off the ground with some much-needed guidance. I feel so incredibly fortunate to have found you and the knowledge base you shared—both in writing and healing. I am thankful for your encouragement and writing advice but also for your compassion and help navigating my emotional struggles. Your impact goes well beyond the book itself.

Thank you, Becky Kollmorgen, for proofreading some of my earliest versions of the manuscript and your thoughtful and honest insights. I still laugh about when we ran into each other before you had an opportunity to fully gather your initial thoughts. I very much enjoyed our one-on-one meetings to discuss the manuscript and dig deeper into the concepts. Thank you, Becky K.

Thank you to my dear friend Mike Duckworth. Your support during some of my most difficult moments had more impact on me than you will ever know. As did the honest feedback you provided after reviewing my manuscript. Your patience, listening skills, and compassion are things I admire so much.

Thank you, Tina Welling of Jackson, Wyoming. How lucky was I to be able to have found you in Wyoming—your presence in a place I love to be. Your feedback on my book as well as the confidence and knowledge you gave me to find a publisher is received with much gratitude.

You each read *My Pain-Body Solution* way before it was ready or even had a name, and because of that you played a major role in moving it forward. All four of you are part of this book—thank you!

Thank you to all my teachers and healers I have met along the way. Words really can't accurately describe what you each mean to me.

Thank you, Dr. Stracks, for your guidance and commitment to bringing awareness to the effects of the mind-body connection. The dedication and service you provide your patients are what doctors should emulate. You are truly a healer!

Thank you, Dr. Eric Sherman, for allowing me to feel comfortable as I explored my inner world. Without that, I can't imagine I would be where I am today.

And with deep bows, an eternal thank you to Kali Basman. You were simply a gift to me, and a treasure to humanity.

To Mikey, Kaylee, and Jaimie. The love I feel for you and the connection I feel to you runs through the core of my soul. The spirit in each of you always shone brightest during my darkest days. Thank you for being there for me. And thank you for the support and encouragement you provided while I wrote this book. Your youthful enthusiasm for the project was ever so contagious.

To my wife, Becky, I most want to thank you. Thank you for the love, patience, and encouragement (and the very large swath you gave me to play in the mountains). Not to mention the countless hours you spent reading my manuscript (albeit painfully slowly) on demand and providing me with critical feedback. Your support never faltered. My partner in life's journey, you are the anchor that keeps our family grounded. You are an amazing parent and I have learned so much from you—the value of kindness is on top of that list.

Resources

Medicine and Trauma

1. *Explain Pain* and *The Explain Pain Handbook Protectometer* by David Butler and G. Lorimer Moseley

2. *Waking the Tiger: Healing Trauma* by Peter Levine

3. *Healing Back Pain: The Mind-Body Connection* by John Sarno

4. *The Body Keeps the Score* by Bessel van der Kolk

5. *When the Body Says No* by Gabor Mate

6. *The Deepest Well: Healing the Long-Term Effects of Childhood Trauma and Adversity* by Nadine Burke Harris

7. *Nurturing Resilience: Helping Clients Move Forward from Developmental Trauma—An Integrative Somatic Approach* by Kathy L. Kain and Stephen J. Terrell

Spiritual

1. *The Power of Now* by Eckhart Tolle

2. *The Surrender Experiment* by Michael A. Singer

3. *The Untethered Soul: The Journey Beyond Yourself* by Michael A. Singer

4. *Feelings Buried Alive Never Die* by Karol K. Truman

5. *Revolution of the Soul: Awaken to Love through Raw Truth, Radical Healing, and Conscious Action* by Seane Corn

Buddhism

1. *Reconciliation: Healing the Inner Child* by Thich Nhat Hanh

2. *When Things Fall Apart: Heart Advice for Difficult Times* by Pema Chödrön

3. *The Joy of Living: Unlocking the Secret and Science of Happiness* by Yongey Mingyur Rinpoche

4. *The Heart of the Buddha's Teaching: Transforming Suffering into Peace, Joy, and Liberation* by Thich Nhat Hanh

5. *Real Love: The Art of Mindful Connection* by Sharon Salzberg

6. *Eastern Body, Western Mind: Psychology and the Chakra System as a Path to the Self* by Anodea Judith

7. *The Buddha's Way of Happiness: Healing Sorrow, Transforming Negative Emotion & Finding Well-Being in the Present Moment* by Thomas Bien

8. *Radical Acceptance: Embracing Your Life with the Heart of a Buddha* by Tara Brach

Suggested YouTube Watches

1. *Finding Joe*, 2011, full movie

2. Dr. Gabor Mate

3. Dr. Peter Levine

4. Dr. Bessel Van der Kolk

5. Eckhart Tolle

6. Thich Nhat Hanh

7. Tara Brach

8. Ram Das (also Spotify top songs)

9. Irene Lyon

Professional Resources

1. Dr. John Stracks
   www.drstracks.com
   312-489-8890
   info@drstracks.com

2. Eric Sherman, PsyD
   19 West 34th Street
   Suite PH-13
   New York, NY 10001
   esherman@pathwaystopainrelief.com
   https://pathwaystopainrelief.com

3. Kali Basman
   www.kalidurgayoga.com
   kali.basman@gmail.com

4. Curable Health
   www.curablehealth.com

About the Author

MICHAEL JAMES MURRAY was born and grew up in Sudbury, Massachusetts. After graduating college in 1988, he spent the following year living as a ski bum in Aspen, Colorado. Upon returning from the Rockies, he moved to New Hampshire. In 2007, at the age of forty-three, he retired after he and his two business partners built and sold a successful financial service business.

He lives in North Hampton, New Hampshire, is married, and has three grown children. He is an avid outdoorsman and loves to backcountry ski, fly-fish, hike, cycle, and surf. He has a second home in Wilson, Wyoming, at the base of the Tetons where he resides part of the year, pursuing his passions.

My Pain-Body Solution is Michael Murray's first book.